OPPOSING
VIEWPOINTS®
SERIES

| Genetic Disorders

Other Books of Related Interest:

Opposing Viewpoints Series

Genetic Engineering

At Issue Series

Are Adult Stem Cells as Valuable as Embryonic Stem Cells?

Current Controversies Series

Alternative Therapies

"Congress shall make no law . . . abridging the freedom of speech, or of the press."

First Amendment to the U.S. Constitution

The basic foundation of our democracy is the First Amendment guarantee of freedom of expression. The Opposing Viewpoints Series is dedicated to the concept of this basic freedom and the idea that it is more important to practice it than to enshrine it.

OPPOSING VIEWPOINTS® SERIES

Genetic Disorders

Katherine Swarts, Book Editor

GREENHAVEN PRESS
A part of Gale, Cengage Learning

Detroit • New York • San Francisco • New Haven, Conn • Waterville, Maine • London

Christine Nasso, *Publisher*
Elizabeth Des Chenes, *Managing Editor*

For more information, contact:
Greenhaven Press
27500 Drake Rd.
Farmington Hills, MI 48331-3535
Or you can visit our Internet site at gale.cengage.com

For product information and technology assistance, contact us at

Gale Customer Support, 1-800-877-4253
For permission to use material from this text or product, submit all requests online at
www.cengage.com/permissions

Further permissions questions can be emailed to permissionrequest@cengage.com

Articles in Greenhaven Press anthologies are often edited for length to meet page requirements. In addition, original titles of these works are changed to clearly present the main thesis and to explicitly indicate the author's opinion. Every effort is made to ensure that Greenhaven Press accurately reflects the original intent of the authors. Every effort has been made to trace the owners of copyrighted material.

Cover photograph © Rolffimage/Dreamtime.com.

LIBRARY OF CONGRESS CATALOGING-IN-PUBLICATION DATA

Genetic disorders / Katherine Swarts, book editor.
    p. cm. -- (Opposing viewpoints)
    Includes bibliographical references and index.
    ISBN 978-0-7377-4212-1 (hardcover)
    ISBN 978-0-7377-4213-8 (pbk.)
    1. Genetic disorders--Popular works. I. Swarts, Katherine.
    RB155.5.G4544 2009
    616'.042--dc22

                                     2008053249

Printed in the United States of America
1 2 3 4 5 6 7 13 12 11 10 09

Contents

Chapter 3: What Should Be Done to Address Genetic Disorders?

Why Consider Opposing Viewpoints?

> "The only way in which a human being can make some approach to knowing the whole of a subject is by hearing what can be said about it by persons of every variety of opinion and studying all modes in which it can be looked at by every character of mind. No wise man ever acquired his wisdom in any mode but this."
>
> John Stuart Mill

In our media-intensive culture it is not difficult to find differing opinions. Thousands of newspapers and magazines and dozens of radio and television talk shows resound with differing points of view. The difficulty lies in deciding which opinion to agree with and which "experts" seem the most credible. The more inundated we become with differing opinions and claims, the more essential it is to hone critical reading and thinking skills to evaluate these ideas. Opposing Viewpoints books address this problem directly by presenting stimulating debates that can be used to enhance and teach these skills. The varied opinions contained in each book examine many different aspects of a single issue. While examining these conveniently edited opposing views, readers can develop critical thinking skills such as the ability to compare and contrast authors' credibility, facts, argumentation styles, use of persuasive techniques, and other stylistic tools. In short, the Opposing Viewpoints Series is an ideal way to attain the higher-level thinking and reading skills so essential in a culture of diverse and contradictory opinions.

In addition to providing a tool for critical thinking, Opposing Viewpoints books challenge readers to question their own strongly held opinions and assumptions. Most people form their opinions on the basis of upbringing, peer pressure, and personal, cultural, or professional bias. By reading carefully balanced opposing views, readers must directly confront new ideas as well as the opinions of those with whom they disagree. This is not to simplistically argue that everyone who reads opposing views will—or should—change his or her opinion. Instead, the series enhances readers' understanding of their own views by encouraging confrontation with opposing ideas. Careful examination of others' views can lead to the readers' understanding of the logical inconsistencies in their own opinions, perspective on why they hold an opinion, and the consideration of the possibility that their opinion requires further evaluation.

Evaluating Other Opinions

To ensure that this type of examination occurs, Opposing Viewpoints books present all types of opinions. Prominent spokespeople on different sides of each issue as well as well-known professionals from many disciplines challenge the reader. An additional goal of the series is to provide a forum for other, less known, or even unpopular viewpoints. The opinion of an ordinary person who has had to make the decision to cut off life support from a terminally ill relative, for example, may be just as valuable and provide just as much insight as a medical ethicist's professional opinion. The editors have two additional purposes in including these less known views. One, the editors encourage readers to respect others' opinions—even when not enhanced by professional credibility. It is only by reading or listening to and objectively evaluating others' ideas that one can determine whether they are worthy of consideration. Two, the inclusion of such viewpoints encourages the important critical thinking skill of objectively evaluating an author's credentials and bias. This evaluation will illuminate an author's reasons for taking a particular stance on an issue and will aid in readers' evaluation of the author's ideas.

It is our hope that these books will give readers a deeper understanding of the issues debated and an appreciation of the complexity of even seemingly simple issues when good and honest people disagree. This awareness is particularly important in a democratic society such as ours in which people enter into public debate to determine the common good. Those with whom one disagrees should not be regarded as enemies but rather as people whose views deserve careful examination and may shed light on one's own.

Thomas Jefferson once said that "difference of opinion leads to inquiry, and inquiry to truth." Jefferson, a broadly educated man, argued that "if a nation expects to be ignorant and free ... it expects what never was and never will be." As individuals and as a nation, it is imperative that we consider the opinions of others and examine them with skill and discernment. The Opposing Viewpoints Series is intended to help readers achieve this goal.

David L. Bender and Bruno Leone,
Founders

Introduction

"Today's politically-correct, sanitized text-books . . . will ensure the next generation of American utopians will never know [that] the pseudo-science which spawned Adolph Hitler's horrific acts of ethnic cleansing was developed in American laboratories, and upheld by the highest court in the land."

—Center for Individual Freedom,
nonprofit advocacy group, 2002

Long before abortion became a major controversy, there was the question of whether conception should even be allowed if there was risk the fetus would be "imperfect." After Charles Darwin published his theories of evolution and natural selection in the mid-1800s, acceptance of the idea that species could change over time led to the social movement called "eugenics" (meaning, roughly, "good genes"). If the genes most frequently passed from generation to generation determined the future physical characteristics of a species, reasoned social reformers, why not work for the overall improvement of the human race by encouraging the healthiest and most intelligent people to have the most children?

It was a short step to the idea of "weeding out the unfit" by actively keeping what were viewed by some as *less* healthy and intelligent people from reproducing. The United States was the first country to actively pursue compulsory sterilization of people whose genes were deemed undesirable; even President Theodore Roosevelt claimed that "society has no business to permit degenerates to reproduce their kind." Starting with Indiana in 1907, more than half of U.S. states eventually legalized forcible sterilization.

Buck v. Bell

Such operations increased significantly after the 1927 Supreme Court case of *Buck v. Bell*, in which a young woman named Carrie Buck was ordered in an eight-to-one ruling to have her tubes tied because she was considered mentally and morally deficient. Buck had been committed to the Virginia State Colony for Epileptics and Feebleminded after becoming pregnant out of wedlock; the superintendent claimed she had a mental age of nine. Her mother was in a mental institution, while Carrie's daughter, Vivian (three years old at the time of the court decision), was an allegedly "backward" child, seemingly justifying the claim that the mental deficiency must be hereditary.

"It is better for all the world, if instead of waiting to execute degenerate offspring for crime, or to let them starve for their imbecility, society can prevent those who are manifestly unfit from continuing their kind," wrote prominent Justice Oliver Wendell Holmes Jr., in the court's majority decision. "Three generations of imbeciles are enough." So Carrie Buck was kept from ever bearing more children, lest they prove social liabilities. (Her daughter and sister were also sterilized, the latter clandestinely under the guise of an appendectomy.)

Eugenics and the Dangers of Discrimination

The *Buck v. Bell* decision gave official endorsement to the idea that the "genetically unfit" should be kept from reproducing. Sterilization rates continued to increase for the next decade and a half. Laws were often so liberally interpreted that anyone suspected of being "inferior" or "deficient" in any way—not only people with inborn mental or physical disabilities, but the sexually promiscuous, anyone convicted of criminal activity, and even members of ethnic minority groups—was at risk of being subjected to forced sterilization.

By the 1940s, support for eugenics had begun to wane. In the 1942 Supreme Court case *Skinner v. Oklahoma*, the court unanimously ruled that Oklahoma's Habitual Criminal Sterilization Act of 1935, which allowed compulsory sterilization for repeat offenders, was unconstitutional because it exempted white-collar felonies. "We have not the slightest basis for inferring ... that the inheritability of criminal traits follows the neat legal distinctions which the law has marked between ... offenses," wrote Justice William O. Douglas. Moreover, "The [very] power to sterilize ... may have subtle, far-reaching and devastating effects. In evil or reckless hands it can cause races or types which are inimical to the dominant group to wither and disappear.... [S]trict scrutiny of the classification which a State makes in a sterilization law is essential, lest ... discriminations are made against groups or types of individuals in violation of the constitutional guaranty of just and equal laws."

Aftermath of the Eugenics Era

Within a few years, Douglas's words would become prophetic as it was revealed that Nazi Germany had not only sterilized its "unfit" citizens by the hundreds of thousands, but had euthanized tens of thousands of others. And Nazi administrators themselves cited U.S. sterilization policies as inspiring their own. By the 1950s, eugenics had lost favor in the United States, though sterilizations continued regularly in some states until the early 1960s. Over sixty-five thousand people would ultimately be forced to sacrifice their fertility in the name of the greater good.

Whether much good was actually accomplished is at best doubtful. Many enforced sterilizations are now known to have been due to bigotry or ignorance rather than any actual genetic abnormalities. The precedent case *Buck v. Bell* is one such; researchers—some of whom interviewed Carrie Buck herself—have concluded that Buck was of normal intelligence;

that her pregnancy was due to rape rather than promiscuity; and that Vivian Buck's school records (Vivian died of an apparently non-genetic illness at age eight) indicate she too was of average or above-average intelligence.

A World of Questions

In any case, scientists now know that inherited traits are a far more complicated matter than once presumed—and today, even known carriers of serious "disorder" genes are rarely discouraged outright from conceiving. But now that doctors can diagnose a variety of genetic disorders in utero, many people worry that fetuses with disorders are aborted too routinely, and that eugenics is returning in a different form. Parents who want to continue pregnancies after disorder diagnoses often feel that public and professional opinion leave little room for the idea that people with disorders have any place in society. *Opposing Viewpoints: Genetic Disorders* addresses this and many other issues in the following chapters: How Serious a Problem Do Genetic Disorders Present? Is Society Accepting of People with Genetic Disorders? What Should Be Done to Address Genetic Disorders? and What Is the Medical Future of Genetic Disorders?

CHAPTER 1

How Serious a Problem Do Genetic Disorders Present?

Chapter Preface

What, exactly, causes genetic disorders? The obvious response, "genes," is overly simplistic. Not everyone with a disorder has a parent who can be diagnosed as a "carrier" of a specific gene that causes the problem; many genetic disorders lack evident regard for bloodlines.

"Some birth defects appear to be caused by a combination of one or more genes and environmental exposures," reports the March of Dimes Foundation, one of the most prominent organizations fighting genetic disorders and other disabilities in newborns. "In some cases, an individual may inherit one or more genes that make him more likely to have a birth defect if he is exposed to certain environmental substances (such as cigarette smoke). . . . But if the individual is not exposed to the environmental substance before birth, he probably won't have the birth defect." Underscoring the difficulty of determining exactly what causes many disorders, the March of Dimes also notes that "the [exact] causes of about 70 percent of birth defects are unknown."

One thing that is known for certain is that many genetic disorders are due to abnormalities of the basic human chromosomal arrangement, rather than to any specific "bad gene." Down syndrome, which manifests itself when someone is born with an extra (or partial) copy of a specific chromosome, is a classic example. But the exact influences, biological or environmental, that cause such abnormalities remain undiscovered.

Many commentators lay blame on environmental factors—specifically, the numerous toxins and food additives modern society is exposed to, many of which may influence genetic mutations. Overfluoridated drinking water, for example, is "cited in research papers as a cause of . . . increasing genetic disorders," reported England's Surrey Green Party in 2003.

And British journalist Maggie O'Kane, researching the afteref-fects of the 1991 Persian Gulf War in which "planes fired at least 1 million rounds of ammunition coated in a radioactive material known as depleted uranium," noted an enormous in-crease of birth defects in Iraq during the 1990s. O'Kane quotes Iraqi geneticist Selma al-Taha, who said, "Something has hap-pened to the environment since the war. . . . Radiation is most effective on a fast-changing organism like a fetus. . . . We're getting mothers as young as twenty giving birth to [babies with Down syndrome—generally a disorder associated with late-thirties and older pregnancies]."

The possible causes of genetic disorders may be innumer-able, but researchers will no doubt continue to probe for an-swers. This chapter explores some of the questions surround-ing the causes and extent of genetic disorders and the effects of these disorders on society and individuals.

"[The worldwide incidence of genetic birth defects] is a serious, vastly unappreciated and underfunded public health problem." (Dr. Jennifer Howse, president, March of Dimes)

Genetic Birth Defects Are More Common than Formerly Thought

Lee Bowman

In the following viewpoint, Lee Bowman reports on the first worldwide study of genetic disorder prevalence. Directed by the March of Dimes Foundation, a major nonprofit organization for the prevention of birth defects, the study concluded that genetic disorders constitute a "largely hidden epidemic" affecting about 8 million newborns a year, and recommends measures to reduce incidents. Other health articles Bowman has written or co-authored for major distributor Scripps Howard News Service include "Going Ape: Even Legally Sober Drinkers Miss the Obvious," "Saving Babies: Exposing Sudden Infant Death in America," and "New Research Shows Stark Differences in Teen Brains."

Lee Bowman, "A Hidden Epidemic of Birth Defects," *Scripps Howard News Service*, January 31, 2006. SHNS © United Feature Syndicate, Inc. Distributed by United Feature Syndicate, Inc.

As you read, consider the following questions:

1. According to the March of Dimes, genetic disorders kill how many children under five each year?
2. What five genetic-linked conditions account for more than one in four birth defects incidents?
3. By what percentage have birth defects in the United States been reduced over the past forty years?

There's a largely hidden epidemic of birth defects running through the world's infants and children, striking about 8 million every year, about 6 percent of those born, according to a new study.

An estimated 3.3 million children under age 5 die from a serious birth defect of genetic or partially genetic origin, while another 3.2 million of those who survive are mentally or physically disabled for life, researchers from the March of Dimes reported Monday [January 30, 2006].

It is the first global effort to calculate the toll.

Estimates are based on data from the relatively few countries where birth defects have been well-documented and where projections based on the demographics, economies and cultures of those where conditions are less well-recognized. Those estimates show that the vast majority of the impact from birth defects is felt in middle- and low-income countries.

The report does not attempt to calculate the hundreds of thousands more infants born each year with birth defects caused by exposure during pregnancy to environmental toxins, alcohol, tobacco smoke and diseases such as rubella and syphilis.

The March of Dimes Goes International

The March of Dimes—an advocate for ending birth defects in this country [the United States] since 1938—went international in 1998 to help set up a global alliance of organizations dedicated to preventing and correcting birth defects. The new report is part of a concerted effort to place birth defects on the public health agenda of national governments and international health organizations.

"This is a serious, vastly unappreciated and underfunded public health problem," said Dr. Jennifer Howse, president of the March of Dimes.

Christopher Howson is an epidemiologist and vice president for Global Programs with the March of Dimes who worked on the report. He said the report's data on 193 countries is still too imprecise to do valid comparisons of birth defect rates between countries, but does allow broad comparisons across regions and among countries of different income levels.

"We can't say from the data we have why the rate in the U.S. is 47.8 per 1,000 births and the rate in the Russian Federation is 42.9, but we do know that there are a lot of factors that are common across national boundaries," Howson said.

The Most Common Birth Defects

In addition to addressing poverty and the health problems that go with it, the report notes there are significant demographic reasons why poorer nations have higher birth-defect rates. They include: more women of advanced age having children and a greater frequency of marriages between individuals who are close blood relatives.

Five common defects of genetic or partially genetic origin accounted for about 26 percent of such birth defects in 2001: congenital heart defects (more than 1 million), neural tube defects (324,000), Down syndrome (218,000), hemoglobin disorders called thalassemia and sickle cell disease (308,000) and another blood-related defect called G6PD deficiency (177,000).

"There are a lot of misperceptions around the world about birth defects, including that they're a problem only rich na-

Birth Defects in Developing Countries

More than 4 million children are born with birth defects each year. There is little doubt that birth defects cause enormous harm in settings where risk factors for many conditions are elevated and resources for health care are limited. . . .

Although individually rare, birth defects taken together account for a significant proportion of morbidity and mortality among infants and children, particularly in areas where infant mortality due to more common causes has been reduced. The prevalence of specific conditions varies widely in different populations. In countries where basic public health services are not available, the birth prevalence of serious birth defects is generally higher than in developed countries.

Judith R. Bale, Barbara J. Stoll, Adetokunbo O. Lucas,
and Institute of Medicine (U.S.) Committee on
Improving Birth Outcomes, Reducing Birth Defects:
Meeting the Challenge in the Developing World, *2004.*

tions can afford to address or that only countries with sophisticated health care systems can make any progress," Howson said.

Many birth defects aren't recognized or considered a cause of death in nations where young children die so readily from infectious diseases, the report says. Even in the most developed nations, only about 50 percent of birth defects are accurately diagnosed.

Yet, "with some relatively low-tech interventions and training that we're advocating in the report, a lot of improvement could be attained," Howson said.

How to Reduce Genetic Birth Defects

Among the proposed interventions: folic acid supplementation to prevent neural tube defects, such as spina bifida; iodination of salt to prevent congenital hypothyroidism; and rubella vaccinations to prevent a congenital rubella syndrome.

"Experience from high-income countries shows that overall mortality and disability from birth defects could be reduced by up to 70 percent if the recommendations in this report were broadly implemented," said Dr. Arnold Christianson of the National Health Lab Service and University of the Witwatersrand in Johannesburg, South Africa.

Howson noted that many middle-income nations have birth defect rates roughly equivalent to those found in the United States in 1960, which have been reduced by 62 percent over the past four decades.

Other interventions proposed by the report include educating health workers, political leaders and the general public in each country about the toll of birth defects and the risk factors that might be changed to avoid them, such as having children at older ages and intermarriage.

Moreover, Howson said, general education in medical genetics would not only help various countries curb birth defects, but could help poorer nations tap into the promising fields of genetic testing for disease risk and the tailoring of medicines according to genetic profiles.

"We have every reason to be hopeful that we can reach a day when all babies are born free of birth defects and developmental disabilities."

Nonprofit Organizations Can Have a Positive Impact on Genetic Disorders

Richard H. Carmona

The following viewpoint is excerpted from a 2003 speech, delivered by then Surgeon General of the United States Richard H. Carmona, at a conference of the March of Dimes, one of the leading organizations dedicated to preventing birth defects. Expressing confidence that genetic disorders and other birth defects will someday be eradicated, Carmona focuses on the top priorities—including health literacy, the elimination of racial disparities, and advances in genome research—to be pursued toward that end. Besides serving as Surgeon General from 2002 to 2006, Carmona is a former Army Special Forces medic and hospital chief executive.

Richard H. Carmona, "The March of Dimes and the U.S. Department of Health and Human Services: Partners in Preventing Birth Defects and Infant Mortality," *March of Dimes Volunteer Leadership Conference*, Washington, DC, October 17, 2003. Reproduced by permission.

As you read, consider the following questions:

1. According to Carmona, what is health literacy?
2. According to Carmona, how many "chemical letters" make up the human genome?
3. Research by the Centers for Disease Control and Prevention reports that the average life span of African Americans with Down syndrome is how many years? How many for white Americans? Other racial groups?

I want to thank all of you on behalf of my bosses President [George W.] Bush and Secretary [of Health and Human Services Tommy] Thompson for your leadership in preventing birth defects and reducing infant mortality. The March of Dimes continues to be one of our most important and effective partners. . . .

We must keep working until we know what causes all birth defects and how to prevent them. I am grateful that science is moving us forward quickly. Think of this: 50 years ago, we didn't know what DNA was. Today, we are already beginning to screen genetic information and target appropriate interventions to help people avoid physical and mental conditions and diseases years before their first symptoms would have otherwise appeared. Someday, simply by altering the genotype of a host, an organ will resist disease or heal itself. Someday, we will look back and only *remember* when we worried about birth defects. . . .

The Three Top Health Priorities

When President Bush and Secretary Thompson nominated me to be Surgeon General, they asked me to focus on three priorities to maintain and improve the health of the American people. The President and Secretary insist that the best science always guide our [health] policies and what I do. All three of my priorities are very strongly evidence-based. They are:

- First, *Prevention.* What each of us can do in our own lives and communities to make ourselves and our families healthier.

- Second, and new to the Office of the Surgeon General, as none of my predecessors had to deal with these issues: *Public Health Preparedness.* We are investing resources at the federal, state, and local levels to prevent, mitigate, and respond to all-hazards emergencies.

- Third, *Eliminating Health Care Disparities.* I am so happy and proud that the President and Secretary charged me with working with them and all of you to eliminate health disparities. Notice that they didn't just charge me with *reducing* health disparities. They said we will *eliminate* health disparities.

Woven through all these three priorities issues is health literacy, what I call the common currency to achieving success in all of those priorities.

Health Literacy and Prevention

We must work together to increase Americans' health literacy.

Health literacy is the ability of an individual to access, understand, and use health-related information and services to make appropriate health decisions. America has the best health care system in the world. Medical discovery is advancing at a rate unequaled in any previous era. Yet many Americans do not know how to use these advances to help their families stay healthy and safe. In fact, many Americans—particularly in communities of color like where I grew up—still don't know about the dangers of drinking alcohol during pregnancy. And many Americans in communities of color don't get the prenatal care they need. It's tragic that nearly 30 percent of American Indian mothers-to-be do not receive any prenatal care in their first trimester. The good news is that because of

Worldwide Developments in Genetic Disorder Prevention

In the last few decades medicine has begun to focus on prevention in developing countries. Priority was given to infectious disease prevention, to immunization and to prevention of child malnutrition; that contributed hugely to the implementation of several kinds of programmes in this field. These programmes succeeded partially or entirely in some countries while acute health problems are still present in other countries. . . . Families could avoid recurrences of disorders that had already occurred. Amniocenteses for fetal chromosome anomaly diagnosis was reported first in 1967.

Today genetic facilities are widespread in developed countries. Genetic counselling and prevention of hereditary, congenital, and common diseases of adulthood are available for these populations. In developing countries, genetic services are still rare and absent in some countries. The prevention of genetic disorders could be effective at two levels:

- General population.
- Families and individuals at risk.

Health education programs improve health, identify and reduce disease risks, manage chronic illness, and improve the well-being and self-sufficiency of individuals, families, organizations, and communities.

"Genetic Counselling and Prevention of Genetic Disorders:
A Myth or Reality in Developing Countries?"
European Genetics Foundation, March 14, 2008. www.charite.de.

the availability of Medicaid, more women than ever are receiving prenatal care and education.

We must do more to increase Americans' health literacy. To do that, we need your help. What the March of Dimes has done to increase understanding of the need for folic acid is health literacy at its best. The research that showed how folic acid prevents birth defects was a major step forward in prevention.

Your continued support of this effort will ensure that more women get the folic acid message, and that more children are born healthy. Again, the power of health literacy. . . .

The Future of Life

The next area for progress is in genetics, genomics, and proteomics [the study of protein structures and functions]. Scientists are nearly finished mapping the human genome's three billion chemical letters—this work will have untold benefits throughout the future of humanity. Already, researchers have identified "susceptibility" genes for disease states, including many cancers.

Now, for the first time, the human genome project has provided us with the basis for a new technology called microarrays. This will allow us to compare the active genes from pregnant women who begin labor prematurely with genes from women who deliver their babies at full term.

This comparison will help us to identify the gene products that are responsible for initiating labor. Armed with this knowledge, we can learn how to postpone labor. Through science, which you support and nurture, we have within our reach the hope of addressing preterm labor. This is the future of science, and the future of life.

Caring for People with Birth Defects and Developmental Disabilities

We have made extraordinary advances in reducing birth defects in recent decades. But until the day when all babies are born free of birth defects, and when we can prevent the many injuries that result in lifelong disabilities, the number of people living with a disability will continue to grow.

More than 50 million Americans live with a disability today and that number will likely increase to nearly 75 million by the year 2010. Americans with disabilities are living healthier lives, but there are significant disparities among racial and ethnic groups.

One example is the survival of individuals with Down syndrome. A recent CDC [Centers for Disease Control and Prevention] study compared survival of children with Down syndrome in 1967 to 1997. In 1967, the median age of death was 1 year. By 1997 it had reached 50 years. That's truly incredible. But the study found major racial disparities: African American children with Down syndrome survival was 25 years, not the 50 years reported for white children. For children with Down syndrome of other races, the median age of death was even lower, only 11 years. Much research is needed to explain those differences, and HHS [Health and Human Services] is committed to that work.

State and federal education departments spend over $40 billion each year on special education programs for individuals from 3 to 21 years of age. Individuals with disabilities have a greater share of depression, hospitalizations, and less access to health promotion activities—from physical activity to preventive health care, such as mammograms. HHS is funding programs that promote wellness among individuals with disabilities, and these programs work. The people who are enrolled in these programs have fewer hospital visits, and if they are admitted to the hospital, their stay is shorter.

Moving Forward

It is clear that together we have accomplished so much. The science is moving forward, the care systems and infrastructure are in place, and we have every reason to be hopeful that we can reach a day when all babies are born free of birth defects and developmental disabilities.

Because of the March of Dimes and our partnerships with you, we can dream of a day when birth defects no longer occur. It was 50 years ago that [James] Watson and [Francis] Crick discovered the DNA double helix. Look at all we have learned in 50 years. A few months ago, I sat at a table during a dinner at the Library of Congress to celebrate the discovery of DNA. On one side of the table was Dr. James Watson, and at the other side was Dr. Francis Collins [director of the National Human Genome Research Institute until August 2008]. Right before me I had the human genome project, at the same table. That's the way it struck me.

Someday, you won't have to hold this meeting about the problem of birth defects. Science will have solved this problem, just as you helped science eliminate polio.

All of us—government, academia, health care professionals, corporations, and communities—need to work together to join this quest to eliminate birth defects and developmental disabilities.

> "[Our] study indicated that siblings of children with ASD [autistic spectrum disorder] are at an increased risk of developing [and] internalising behaviour problems."

Siblings of Children with Genetic Disorders May Develop Behavioral Problems

Penelope Ross and Monica Cuskelly

The following selection reports on a behavioral study of families that include children with autistic spectrum disorder (ASD)— which many researchers believe is genetically linked—and children without ASD, focusing specifically on non-ASD siblings. Conclusions include that nearly half of the non-ASD children had some sort of behavioral problem; that ASD-related aggression is the most common stress factor; and that emotional control and wishful thinking are frequently used coping strategies. Both authors are affiliated with the School of Education at the

Penelope Ross and Monica Cuskelly, "Adjustment, Sibling Problems and Coping Strategies of Brothers and Sisters of Children with Autistic Spectrum Disorder," *Journal of Intellectual & Developmental Disability*, vol. 31, June 2006, pp. 77–86. Copyright © 2006 Australasian Society for the Study of Intellectual Disability Inc. Reprinted by permission of Taylor & Francis, Ltd., http//:www.tandf.co.uk/journals, conveyed through Copyright Clearance Center, Inc., and the authors.

University of Queensland in Australia; Monica Cuskelly, an associate professor of education, has significant experience researching Down syndrome and how disabilities affect families.

As you read, consider the following questions:

1. According to the authors, autistic spectrum disorder (ASD) encompasses what two more specific diagnoses?
2. What factors do the authors admit may have distorted the conclusions of this study?
3. What were found to be the *least* common coping strategies used by non-ASD siblings?

While it has been established that the siblings of children with autistic spectrum disorder (ASD) experience more difficulties in their relationships than do children in families where all children are developing typically, investigation of the day-to-day difficulties experienced by siblings of children with ASD and of how they cope with these stressors has been a relatively neglected area of research. [Dr. Monica] Cuskelly argued in 1999 that research focusing on dynamic aspects of the sibling relationship is more likely to contribute to ameliorating the impact of a child with a disability on their sibling than research into status variables such as age and birth order. Her reasoning was that dynamic variables are open to change and therefore provide the foci for interventions.

The study reported here investigated the impact of two dynamic variables on the adjustment of siblings of children with ASD, namely coping skills and knowledge of ASD. In addition, it examined the types of difficulties reported by brothers and sisters of children with ASD. The term ASD is used to include children with a range of social and communication problems. Often, a more specific diagnosis of autism or Asperger syndrome is made for children on this spectrum. The present study included children with either of these diagnoses. . . .

Coping Strategies for Families

Parents [of children with disabilities] must recognize that their other children often feel torn between protecting and caring for their brother or sister with a disability and being accepted by children outside the family who may tease them and their sibling. Siblings should be informed at an early age about their brother or sister's disability so their knowledge is based on fact, not misconception. This must be done in an age-appropriate fashion, with the siblings feeling free to ask questions. These sessions will need to be repeated as the children grow older and require more information. By the time siblings have reached adolescence, the parents may be ready to share with them information about genetics, estate planning, guardianship arrangements, and wills. It is helpful for siblings to know what resources and options are available. Some siblings will choose to have their sibling with a disability live with them in the future or they may promote their sibling's independence by finding living arrangements and/or the available systems of care in their community. The family should stay current with services offered in their community as well as be aware of any waiting lists for those services.

Symme Wilson Trachtenberg, Karen Batshaw,
and Michael Batshaw, "Caring and Coping:
Helping the Family of a Child with a Disability,"
Children with Disabilities. *6th ed. Baltimore, MD:*
Paul H. Brookes Publishing, 2007.

Significant Adjustment Problems

Although the mean [average] levels of internalising and exter-nalising behaviour scores were well within the normal range for the participating sibling group, 40% of the siblings were reported by their mother to have significant adjustment problems, predominantly internalising difficulties. The current findings are consistent with [the research of N.] Gold, who noted in 1993 clinical levels of depression in adolescent siblings of children with autism, and with [that of Sandra] Fisman and colleagues, who identified significantly higher levels of internalising and externalising behaviour problems in siblings of children with Pervasive Developmental Disorder over a 3-year period. [Susan L.] Smalley et al. also found an increased rate of major depressive disorders among siblings of individuals with autism, and suggested that the familial link of autism and depressive disorders could be due to shared genetic underpinnings. With the knowledge that the incidence of autism increases markedly in first-degree relatives, it is possible that male siblings are at an increased genetic vulnerability for developing adjustment difficulties. It is important to keep in mind, however, that the sample included in the study reported here was small, included only English-speakers, and may therefore be unrepresentative. The fact that the sample was comprised of volunteers may also contribute to bias, with parents who were concerned about the participating sibling's adjustment being more likely to agree to take part in the study.

Aggression Is a Major Stressor

Aggresion was identified as the most common type of stressor within the sibling interaction, with 84% of participating siblings reporting it as a concern. Furthermore, 52% of participating siblings reported aggressive behaviours as a problem on the first occasion when they were asked to identify a problem they were having with their sibling. This is consistent with [the research of A.] Bågenholm and [C.] Gillberg, who found in 1991 that a disproportionate number of siblings of children with autism reported problems with their sibling disturbing them and breaking their property. However, due to the lack of a comparative sample of siblings of typically developing children, it is unclear whether the predominance of aggressive problems in the dyad is specific to families with a child with ASD. Aggressive behaviour may well reflect typical sibling relationships and interactions. Further examination with an appropriate comparison group is required to determine whether it is particularly characteristic of sibling interactions in families with a child with ASD. Not surprisingly, anger was found to be the strongest emotional reaction to aggressive behaviours. The fact that two-thirds of the group provided more than one type of problem when given the opportunity points to a limitation of the *Kidcope* [a screening measure of childhood coping strategies] in identifying the range of problems experienced by the group.

Not Problem Specific

Choice of coping strategies did not appear to be problem specific. Participating siblings' reported use of coping strategies was very similar across aggressive and syndrome-specific incidents. Emotional regulation and wishful thinking were the most common strategies for both types of problem. The least common coping strategies were blaming others (24% and 8% respectively) and self-criticism (10% and 17% respectively). The finding that emotional regulation was the most frequently used strategy in response to aggression is interesting, as anger was the strongest emotional response to aggressive behaviours. It is possible that siblings of children with ASD are aware of the level of anger that aggressive behaviours produce in them and choose to cope with the situation by actively controlling their emotions. The equally high level of wishful thinking suggests that siblings of children with ASD have a strong desire for things to be different. . . .

The current study indicated that siblings of children with ASD are at an increased risk of developing internalising behaviour problems. The contributing factors to this outcome are unknown and may include a genetic predisposition. It is important for future research to focus on dynamic variables in the search for these contributors since, by definition, they are open to change.

| "All the things I had surrendered hope of ever doing with my son were still attainable; they were just waiting for the right time."

Families May Find Hope Through Children with Genetic Disorders

John C. McGinley as told to Tom Groneberg

In the following viewpoint, actor John C. McGinley reviews the early days with his son, Max, who has Down syndrome—the shock at the birth; the health issues; and the "huge forfeiture of desire and expectations"—and goes on to discuss recent progress, present joys, and hopes for the future. McGinley is best known for his role as Dr. Cox on the medical sitcom Scrubs. *Tom Groneberg is a health and outdoor writer whose works include "Why Our Burgers Still Aren't Safe" (*Men's Health, *February 2008) and* The Secret Life of Cowboys.

As you read, consider the following questions:

1. What major news event did McGinley hardly notice on his son's birth date?

2. At what age did Max begin to suffer from seizures?

3. What does McGinley refer to as "the great comeback story"?

My son, Max, was born the day Princess Di [Diana of England] died [August 31, 1997]. Lauren, Max's mother, and I didn't know why everyone was in shock, but we knew why we were. During her pregnancy, Lauren didn't have an amnio, but all the blood tests and sonograms came back okay. Everything was thumbs-up for us to have a little girl. When a little boy came out instead, that was fine. But 20 minutes later, the doctor told us that Max had Down syndrome. I didn't know what Down syndrome was, not a clue.

At first I just wanted to take on his problems, just give them to me instead of this little newborn. Then this crazy blame game started, and I wondered what I had done to cause this. There wasn't any family history; it made no sense. Turns out, Down syndrome is the most common genetic disorder, occurring once in every 800 births, and no one really knows why it happens. It just does.

Getting an Education

There's a song on Paul Simon's *Graceland* album that goes, "Breakdowns come and breakdowns go, so what are you gonna do about it?" Eventually, I got my head out of the sand and realized I needed to step up. I took about a year off from acting. Lauren and I attended seminars on Down syndrome, read everything we could get our hands on, and looked into the different kinds of therapies. Max avoided the heart issues and digestive problems that babies with Down syndrome are prone to, but the damned seizures took hold of him when he was 3.

These weren't grand real seizures, but rather something that would build and then trigger a momentary shutdown. During the seizures, he also had sleep apnea, so the doctors hooked Max up to a monitor that would go off if he stopped breathing for more than 15 seconds. It gave off this ear-

A Down Syndrome Family

[Quoting the mother of Mark Radel, a toddler with Down syndrome:] [Our older son] Luke always wants to help with Mark's therapies. . . . There's nothing nicer than when my husband and I see Luke put his arm around Mark and say, "You're my best friend, Mark. I love you." . . .

There are different struggles and worries that my husband and I have with Mark than we had with Luke. But there are also different rewards and joys. . . .

Mark's having Down syndrome has forced us to focus on the fundamentals—what's really important in life.

Christine M. Porretta,
"Real Family: Raising a Child with Down Syndrome,"
American Baby, July 2008.

piercing sound that would make you want to cling to the ceiling like a cat. We could either wait for the seizures to cycle through on their own, or we could inject Max in the thighs and buttocks with drugs that would accelerate the cycle.

Living Day by Day

When your child stops breathing 60 times a night, you don't worry about what's going on next year or even next week. You put aside thoughts about which preschool you're going to enroll him in and focus on how he's doing right now. It's not the Norman Rockwell relationship that you sign on for when becoming a parent. I began to gear down my expectations for Max. Here was a kid who already had special needs and challenges, and now he was being set back even more. It seemed horribly unfair. I came to understand that my son would do things on his own terms and at his own speed. I resigned myself to the fact that there wouldn't be a lot of games of catch between us. But just because I gave up hoping for such things doesn't mean I didn't miss them. It was a huge forfeiture of desire and expectations.

After about six months, Max's seizures abated, and it took him a year to reacclimatize. Ever since, his progress has been amazing. He's in the top percentile for growth for his age. He's 10 years old, and he just started third grade at an inclusive program at a mainstream school. His math and reading abilities are fantastic. Outside of school, Max is always bouncing on the trampoline or swimming: He's just this great big glorious kid.

The First Game of Catch

Last summer, Max and I often went to the beach in Malibu [California] with our dogs. I'd bring a tennis ball for Max to throw to them, and one day he turned around and threw it right to me. I threw it back, he made a nice two-handed catch, and we kept at it. He didn't make a big deal of it, but it caught me completely off guard. To play catch with my son was the defining moment of my life. That ball toss helped me understand that all the things I had surrendered hope of ever doing with my son were still attainable; they were just waiting for the right time. It's the great comeback story. With that one perfect toss, my son had arrived at something I had left behind a long time ago.

Periodical Bibliography

The following articles have been selected to supplement the diverse views presented in this chapter.

Current Science	"Autism Epidemic a Myth?" March 28, 2008.
Centers for Disease Control and Prevention	"Update on Overall Prevalence of Major Birth Defects—Atlanta, Georgia, 1978–2005," *JAMA: The Journal of the American Medical Association*, February 20, 2008.
Eurekalert.org	"Birth Defects: 8 Million Annually Worldwide," January 30, 2006. www.eurekalert.org.
Fertility Weekly	"Greater Incidence of Congenital Malformations and Epigenetic Diseases," April 21, 2008.
Mary and Richard FitzZaland	"A Parent's View of Ohdo Syndrome," *Exceptional Parent*, August 2008.
Li Li	"Alarming Rise in Birth Defects," *Beijing Review*, December 6, 2007.
Richard Monastersky	"Is There an Autism Epidemic?" *Chronicle of Higher Education*, May 11, 2007.
Peter Schuntermann	"The Sibling Experience: Growing Up with a Child Who Has Pervasive Developmental Disorder or Mental Retardation," *Harvard Review of Psychiatry*, May/June 2007.
Sarah Toland	"Good News About Folic Acid & Infants," *Delicious Living*, November 2004.
Melinda Wenner	"Disease for Darwinism," *Scientific American*, February 2008.
Paul Winston	"Genetic Disorders in Search of a Cure," *Business Insurance*, April 10, 2006.

CHAPTER 2

Is Society Accepting of People with Genetic Disorders?

Chapter Preface

Rightly or wrongly, depictions of people with disabilities in film, television, or other media may shape viewers' opinions and enforce stereotypes. Not surprisingly, films that stereotypically depict people with disabilities as ignorant and inferior are widely decried by activists. But even films that have won critical acclaim, such as the 1988 film *Rain Man*, have sometimes come under fire for their portrayal of characters with disabilities. Both issues are worthy of examination. Indeed, films that depict characters with disabilities as unable to function and invoke a sense of pity for the character also play into the kinds of stereotypes that many decry as outmoded.

Benjamin Snow knows about this firsthand. In 2006 the then 19-year-old was one of five winners in a national contest, "Film Your Issue," for his short film, *Thumbs Down to Pity*. His entry was picked from over three hundred entrants, by a panel that included actor George Clooney and then-Senator Barack Obama. The one-minute film condemns the media's portrayal of people with disabilities as deserving the viewer's pity and shows how incorrect and outdated this stereotype is. Snow has cerebral palsy, and the video depicts him performing a number of tasks that anyone might—writing for his college newspaper, paying his bills, and doing karate moves. Snow challenges viewers to look beyond his wheelchair and see a young man succeeding in life and attaining his dreams.

In an article with Bill Reed of the Colorado Springs *Gazette*, Snow comments that Hollywood gets it wrong by portraying "characters with disabilities as unproductive people with lousy lives." To those that might argue that pity isn't such a bad emotion to evoke, he says, "In pitying people, you are showing that one person is better than the other person, and people not like you are not as good as you." With the support of Snow's family and others he has become not only a great student and writer, but also a leader, and his film has inspired many to reevaluate their long-held beliefs and perceptions.

Society has come a long way in the last several decades in recognizing the unique contributions of people with disabilities, but clearly still has a long way to go in seeing past the disability to view the person first. The viewpoints in the following chapter debate how far society has come in accepting people with disabilities, and how much further society has to go in realizing the goal of equality for all.

"People with disabilities slowly and persistently have paved a new way for themselves, allowing society to grow accustomed to seeing them bagging groceries, running flower stands, serving coffee or stocking shelves."

Society Is Becoming More Accepting of Individuals with Genetic Disorders

Susan Brink

In the following viewpoint Susan Brink talks about the increase in employment opportunities for people with Down syndrome and other disorders, focusing primarily on acting jobs in the television and film industries. About one in a hundred members of the Screen Actors Guild now have some form of mental or physical disability, and their annual employment rate is about 33 percent, better than that of the ethnic-minority subgroup. Brink is a health writer on the staff of the Los Angeles Times.

As you read, consider the following questions:

1. Who was the first actor with Down syndrome to play a character with Down syndrome on a prime time television series?

2. According to one casting director, what is "the ultimate goal" in finding the right actor for a part?

3. According to Brink, one-third of disabled actors and 23 percent of non-disabled "actors of color" found some acting work in 2003. What was the percentage for white, non-disabled actors?

Nick Daley, 28, has Prader-Willi Syndrome, a genetic disorder characterized by short stature, low muscle tone and mild retardation. He's also been in 17 films and 11 television shows, including a guest-starring role in last season's [2007] TNT series "Saving Grace."

"If I were a star, I would be on all over the world," he says. "I would be mobbed by fans. People would see my name and get my autograph."

Blair Williamson, 28, is an actor with Down syndrome. He has been in clothing commercials for Macy's, was once murdered in a "CSI" episode and had a nose job on a "Nip/Tuck" episode.

"I love being an actor," he says. "It makes me feel good inside me."

A Growing Number of Developmentally Disabled Actors

Daley and Williamson are among a growing number of people with developmental disabilities—including Down syndrome, autism spectrum disorders, mild retardation and seizure disorders—who want to be in the movies, or on TV. They want to make records, or be in commercials. They want what a lot of people in this town [Los Angeles] want: to be stars.

And some of them are getting close.

Their aspirations are a small part of a sea change in thinking about adults with disabilities since 1973, when California passed landmark legislation known as the Lanterman Act (updated in 1977). It granted services (and funding for [services]) to people with disabilities to let them live as independent a life as possible.

Since that time, people with disabilities slowly and persistently have paved a new way for themselves, allowing society to grow accustomed to seeing them bagging groceries, running flower stands, serving coffee or stocking shelves. "Our constituents want to work, to be active members of society, to earn money," says Dr. Paula Pompa-Craven, vice president of Easter Seals [a major advocacy and support organization for the disabled] Southern California.

People with Disabilities as—People with Disabilities

And over the decades since the Lanterman Act was passed, people with developmental disabilities are not only coming out of hiding, they're also showing up on the big and small screens as casting directors discover the obvious: People with disabilities who have acting talent can actually play people with disabilities.

According to statistics from the Media Access Office, the state's liaison between performers with disabilities and the media, in 2001, the office submitted 1,087 performers' resumes, which resulted in 64 entertainment jobs. In 2002, the office submitted 961 resumes, resulting in 186 hires. Since then, says Gloria Castaneda, the office's program director, staff limitations have prevented updated statistics.

It's still a rough road for the 10% of Screen Actors Guild members who have a disability. But for talent agents such as Carmel Wynne, who places actors with developmental disabilities, this client pool is becoming an easier sell.

"Why shouldn't more people be able to turn on the TV and see people who look like them?" says Media Access Office volunteer Gail Williamson of North Hills [California], Blair Williamson's mother.

Keeping it Real

Probably the easiest casting call is when the role is for a character with a unique physiognomy. "It's a slam dunk with Down syndrome," says Wynne, director of talent at Performing Arts Studio West, a state-funded acting, music, dance and production studio for people with developmental disabilities in Inglewood [California]. She's referring to the classic facial features associated with the syndrome. "More nontraditional disabilities are harder," she says.

Although the viewing public has come to accept story lines about people with disabilities, typically, non-disabled actors get the roles, as in *My Left Foot, As Good As It Gets*, and *Rain Man*. The 1989 television series "Life Goes On" was a breakthrough—a prime time drama about a family with two children, one of whom had Down syndrome. In that show, Chris Burke, an actor with Down syndrome, played Corky Thatcher, the child with Down syndrome.

John Frank Levey, now senior vice president of casting for John Wells Productions [in Burbank, California] worked with Burke—his first experience with an actor with a disability. "Chris Burke came into the network test, a dehumanizing experience for any actor," Levey says. "Rather than being disarmed, he disarmed everybody and went around the room giving hugs."

The Value of Authenticity

Over the years, Levey has cast actors who are deaf, blind, HIV-positive and developmentally disabled, with an eye on keeping it real. "Authenticity is an important part of good film and television," he says.

Levey cast Nick [Nicholas] Weiland, 29, who has Down syndrome and is a Performing Arts Studio West client, in the role of [actor] Peter Fonda's son in an "ER" episode last season [2007]. Levey was impressed with the actor. "Nicholas was a delight on the set," he says. "He was prepared, open and flexible. He was an actor."

Just last week, another actor who trained at Performing Arts Studio West, Luke Zimmerman, 29, scored a coup—four episodes in an as-yet-untitled ABC Family network project [began airing as "The Secret Life of the American Teenager" in July 2008] created by Brenda Hampton, creator and executive producer for the TV drama "7th Heaven." The new project auditioned non-disabled actors for the role of a disabled older brother in a drama about a family of teenagers but ended up casting Zimmerman, who has Down syndrome, for the recurring role soon after he read, according to John Paizis, founder and director of the acting studio.

Making a Dream Come True

For Nick Daley, acting has been a dream since he was a kid. He watched hundreds of TV shows and movies, imagining himself in countless roles. "When I was 10 or 11, I would imitate the people," he says. His goal was to become a professional actor, and his training at the studio, along with industry connections cultivated by Wynne, helped him snag his TV and movie roles.

"Nick was incredibly professional," says Liz Dean, casting director for the "Saving Grace" episode in which Daley worked with Oscar-winning actress Holly Hunter, the series' lead. "A lot of times actors will come in—these are actors without disabilities—who haven't memorized their lines, haven't made strong choices about the characters.

"Nick came with very strong choices about how the character was feeling at each moment. When I brought him in to read in front of the producers, he was even stronger. Rarely do you see someone get better for the producers. He's an actor who is well trained."

The Advantages of a Disability

The ultimate goal for a casting director, Dean says, is finding the best actor for the role without regard to the performer's personal circumstances. Actors with disabilities have certain advantages in playing characters with similar disabilities. They don't have to worry about how to portray the actual physical or mental challenges. "They live it every day. So they can just act the role," she says. "It's always better to start with the actual disability. Otherwise, there's something that rings false."

In "Saving Grace" Daley played a mentally challenged young man with epilepsy who's suspected of murder. "I wasn't myself," he says. "I was a different person. It feels like you're on a different planet."

Paizis saw Daley's transformation into the character. "He was playing someone who was more low functioning than he actually is, someone more simplistic," Paizis says. On the set, he watched as Daley took a few minutes to concentrate. "He just put his head down. Paused. When he came up, he was a different guy," he says. "I had goose bumps."

The Trouble with Using "Normal" Actors

Paizis finds it troubling when "normal" actors play a character with a developmental disability. "It's difficult for me to watch," he says. "Almost always, they take on childlike aspects. In reality, these guys [with intellectual disabilities] work very, very hard to maintain an adult persona."

People with a variety of disabilities continue to break new ground, sometimes in ways that startle as they illuminate. Marlee Matlin, a deaf actress who won an Academy Award in 1987 for her role in *Children of a Lesser God*, is a contestant on this season's "Dancing With the Stars," waltzing and fox trotting to a silent, internal beat. But clearly there are limits to appropriate casting, and many performers with certain disabilities will likely play characters who have those disabilities. "It would be very hard to have the idea that Hamlet should be somebody with Down's," Levey says. "But within the realities of the disability, the authenticity moves the crew, moves the other actors and creates a great vibe for the audience."

About One Percent of Actors Now Have Disabilities

It's tough for anyone to break into show business, as shown by a 2003 report by the Screen Actors Guild. About 1,200 of the guild's 120,000 members have a disability of any sort, mental or physical. About one-third of those actors with disabilities reported working in a theatrical or television production that year. That's worse than the 73% of white, non-disabled actors who found work, but better than the 23% of non-disabled actors of color.

Even if the clients at Performing Arts Studio West and other studios don't get their big break, the hard work can have other, very practical benefits, says Gail Williamson, who founded the Web site Down Syndrome in Arts and Media. Her son gets acting training at Born to Act Players, a Valley Glen theater company for performers with or without disabilities. She says he gained self-confidence and improved his speech through his acting career, which began with a Procter & Gamble commercial when he was 10.

Self-confidence is a plus in any job market. "People with disabilities learn some amazing life skills through drama," Williamson says. "They learn body awareness. They learn to stay in the moment. They learn to listen so they respond appropriately. They use their speech. And all of these skills translate into any occupation, any social situation. They learn life skills to become employable people."

The Secrets of Success

That's the goal. People who learn to listen, to show up on time and to speak up for themselves are more successful in jobs and in society, says Mike Danneker, executive director of the Westside Regional Center, part of the state system that funds programs for adults with autism, cerebral palsy and mental retardation. "Our push is to get people trained so they can take the next step to the real world, rather than keeping them in a workshop for 40 years," he says.

That might mean a program that concentrates on social skills or language skills. Or a more sheltered program in which people create jewelry or art to sell. Or it might mean a studio where people hone skills in acting, music and dance.

A few years ago, jobs for people with mental disabilities were largely limited to the fields of food or janitorial services. "Now they're in banks, hospitals, law firms," Danneker says. "We [social services professionals] used to be part of the problem. We thought they couldn't do much because they were, you know, 'retarded.' When we raised the bar, and changed our mentality, they took off. We're not going to have brain surgeons come out of our system. But our folks, even with very low IQs, can do a lot of stuff, if given half a chance."

And given a full chance, dreams soar. "Hopefully," Daley says, "I'll win an Academy Award some day."

> "The armed forces' disability policy [is] flawed by a fundamental misunderstanding about the biology of inherited diseases."

The U.S. Military Practices Genetic Discrimination

Karen Kaplan

Prejudice against genetic disorders and the related genes is a particular problem in the U.S. Armed Forces, which are exempt from genetic anti-discrimination laws, writes Karen Kaplan in the following viewpoint. The risk of unfair discharge has many military doctors hesitant to recommend genetic testing at all. Kaplan is a staff writer, specializing in genetics and stem cells, in the science/medicine department of the Los Angeles Times.

As you read, consider the following questions:

1. How long must a person have served in the military to be eligible for disability benefits if the disability has a genetic component?

2. According to Kaplan, "the uniform code of military justice" requires military personnel to seek treatment only

from military doctors. What consequence might be suffered by a service person who went to a civilian doctor for genetic testing?

3. According to Kaplan, who was the first service person to initiate a legal battle for medical benefits after being discharged for genetic reasons?

Eric Miller's career as an Army Ranger wasn't ended by a battlefield wound, but his DNA.

Lurking in his genes was a mutation that made him vulnerable to uncontrolled tumor growth. After suffering back pain during a tour in Afghanistan, he underwent three surgeries to remove tumors from his brain and spine that left him with numbness throughout the left side of his body.

So began his journey into a dreaded scenario of the genetic age.

Because he was born with the mutation, the Army argued it bore no responsibility for his illness and medically discharged him in 2005 without the disability benefits or health insurance he needed to fight his disease.

"The Army didn't give me anything," said Miller, 28, a seven-year veteran who is training to join the Tennessee Highway Patrol.

While genetic discrimination is banned in most cases throughout the country, it is alive and well in the U.S. military.

The Armed Forces Are Different from Civilian Employers

For more than 20 years, the armed forces have held a policy that specifically denies disability benefits to servicemen and women with congenital or hereditary conditions. The practice would be illegal in almost any other workplace.

There is one exception, instituted in 1999, that grants benefits to personnel who have served eight years.

"You could be in the military and be a six-pack-a-day smoker, and if you come down with emphysema, 'That's OK. We've got you covered,'" said Kathy Hudson, director of the Genetics and Public Policy Center at Johns Hopkins University [in Baltimore, Maryland]. "But if you happen to have a disease where there is an identified genetic contribution, you are screwed."

Representatives from the Pentagon declined multiple requests to discuss the policy.

The regulation appears to have stemmed from an effort to protect the armed services from becoming a magnet for people who knew they would come down with costly genetic illnesses, according to Dr. Mark Nunes, who headed the Air Force Genetics Center's DNA diagnostic laboratory at Keesler Air Force Base in Mississippi.

When Military Members Are Discharged for Genetic Reasons

The threat is almost certainly small. A 1999 military analysis estimated that about 250 service members are discharged each year for health problems involving a genetic component. Disability payments for them would amount to $1.7 million the first year and rise each year after that as more veterans join the rolls. Health care expenditures would have added to the tab.

"Maybe they didn't want to foot the bill for my disability," said Miller, whose rare genetic disease is called Von Hippel-Lindau syndrome. "It's saving money for them. I'm just one less soldier that they have to dish out compensation to."

But the cost for individuals medically discharged can be high. While some eventually receive benefits from Veterans Affairs or private insurers, the policy leaves Miller and others scrambling to find treatment for complex medical conditions at the same time they are reestablishing their lives as civilians without having the benefit of Tricare, the military's health insurance.

"It seems particularly draconian to say, 'Well, you're out with no benefits,' whereas another person with the same injury gets the coverage simply because we don't know there's a gene in there that's causing this," said Alex Capron, a professor who studies health care law, policy and ethics at USC [University of Southern California].

The Roots of Genetic Discrimination Issues

The fear of genetic discrimination coincides with early efforts to decode the human genome more than 25 years ago.

It took no great insight to realize that a complete inventory of life's building blocks would not only revolutionize the practice of medicine, but also mark individuals whose genes put them at risk for myriad diseases.

Congress took action in 1996, banning genetic discrimination in group health plans, and in 2000, President [Bill] Clinton signed an executive order forbidding the practice against the federal government's nearly 2 million civilian employees. Similar laws against genetic discrimination swept through 31 states.

Congress is working to extend the federal law with the Genetic Information Nondiscrimination Act, which would protect people with individual medical policies. The act has passed the House and awaits a vote in the Senate. [It became law in May 2008—see sidebar.]

Even if it becomes law, it will not apply to military personnel.

The Defense Department's original policy did not consider genetics when determining whether a soldier deserved medical retirement, assuming that any disease discovered during service had been incurred in the line of duty.

Prohibiting Employment Discrimination on the Basis of Genetic Information

[The Genetic Information Nondiscrimination Act (GINA)] prohibits, as an unlawful employment practice, an employer, employment agency, labor organization, or joint labor-management committee from discriminating against an employee, individual, or member because of genetic information, including: (1) for an employer, by failing to hire or discharging an employee or otherwise discriminating against an employee with respect to the compensation, terms, conditions, or privileges of employment; (2) for an employment agency, by failing or refusing to refer an individual for employment; (3) for a labor organization, by excluding or expelling a member from the organization; (4) for an employment agency, labor organization, or joint labor-management committee, by causing or attempting to cause an employer to discriminate against a member in violation of this Act; or (5) for an employer, labor organization, or joint labor-management committee, by discriminating against an individual in admission to, or employment in, any program established to provide apprenticeships or other training or retraining.

H.R. 493,
May 21, 2008. www.loc.gov.

There was little reason to consider genetic mutations, since few were known. But by 1986, as scientists associated more sections of DNA with particular diseases, the military declared that it was not responsible for soldiers with "congenital and hereditary" conditions.

Changes in Defense Department Rules

At the urging of the National Human Genome Research Institute [NHGRI], the Defense Department proposed in 1999 that anyone who had served for 180 days be eligible for medical retirement, even if their health problem had a genetic component, said Barbara Fuller, assistant director for ethics at NHGRI, part of the National Institutes of Health.

But the Office of Management and Budget decided on the longer, 8-year term to conform with other military health and retirement guidelines, according to an OMB official.

Some genetic discrimination is unavoidable given the demands of military service, said Nunes, now a geneticist at Ohio State University.

"If you have achondroplasia—if you're a dwarf—you're not eligible for military service," he said. "If you have hereditary hearing loss, you're not eligible for military service. If you have color blindness, you're not eligible to fly an airplane. Obviously, there's genetic discrimination in the military, for good reason."

But Nunes said the armed forces' disability policy was flawed by a fundamental misunderstanding about the biology of inherited diseases.

Only in a few cases, such as Huntington's disease, does a specific mutation in a particular stretch of DNA guarantee the onset of illness.

Triggers for Genetic Related Medical Problems

In most cases, a faulty gene increases an individual's risk of developing a disease, but does not ensure it. Typically, an external event is necessary to trigger the onset of a medical condition.

Such was the case with an Army helicopter gunship pilot who was reassigned to desk duty after she became too pregnant to fly.

Dr. Melissa Fries, an Air Force geneticist who became involved in the case, said the pilot developed a blood clot in her leg—a typical complication of pregnancy that is exacerbated by inactivity.

She was diagnosed with chronic thrombophlebitis [blood clotting], a condition that disqualified her from flying. The pilot, who declined to discuss her case, decided to retire from the Army.

As part of her medical work-up, doctors discovered she had a genetic mutation for Factor V Leiden, which is found in 5% of Caucasians and increases their risk of developing blood clots.

An Army physical evaluation board, which determines disability benefits, denied her claim because of the mutation.

Her military doctors were stunned since her thrombophlebitis was probably caused by her pregnancy and desk job. They downplayed the role of her mutation because 99% of Factor V Leiden carriers never develop blood clots.

Testing Discouraged

Military doctors now discourage their patients from getting potentially life-saving genetic tests, undermining their ability to provide top-notch care.

"If someone called me up with regard to genetic testing, I had to say, 'That might not be something you want to pursue,'" Nunes said. "That's very hard to say."

In her 26 years in the Air Force, Fries said she often dissuaded women from getting tested for the BRCA1 and BRCA2 mutations that dramatically increase their risk of developing breast cancer.

She recalled counseling a 22-year-old soldier whose father had just been diagnosed with Huntington's disease. The soldier had 50–50 odds of developing the disease.

A neurologist at Walter Reed Army Medical Center [in Washington, D.C.] ordered a genetic test for Huntington's, and it turned up positive.

"He was discharged from the military on the basis of the Huntington's disease gene even though, at that level of gene expansion, there was expected to be another 25 years before he would display any symptoms," said Fries, now director of genetics and fetal medicine at Washington Hospital Center in Washington, D.C.

For many in the military, the best course is to simply refuse all genetic tests, even though they may be needed for an accurate diagnosis, she said.

Only Military Doctors Are Allowed

Getting genetic tests through civilian channels is not an option because it would violate the uniform code of military justice.

"You could get court-martialed if it were revealed that you had sought medical treatment or testing outside the system," Nunes said.

Most soldiers have no idea about the genetic rule, much less have a reason to challenge it. For those who choose to fight, it can be an arduous process.

No one contested the policy until Marine Gunnery Sgt. Jay Platt did in 1998.

Platt had lost an eye and a testicle to Von Hippel-Lindau syndrome before doctors told him he had a malignant tumor in his left kidney and four benign tumors on his brain. He knew his 15-year Marine career was over.

"If you want to go ahead and medically retire me, I'm not going to fight it," he told his doctors.

But the Marines refused. Instead, he was medically discharged without any benefits because his genetic disease was a preexisting condition.

A discharge would have cut Platt off from Tricare, which allows members to seek care from a large network of providers, just like a civilian HMO.

"That was my biggest thing," he said. "I needed to have treatments for the rest of my life."

Fighting the System

With the help [of] experts from NHGRI, Platt appealed his case to a physical evaluation board. His doctors said that although the mutation predisposed him to Von Hippel-Lindau syndrome, some aspect of his service—such as repeated exposure to the solvents used to clean weapons—could have triggered the tumors.

Platt ultimately won his case and was granted disability payments of about $2,000 a month. He now travels the country as a motivational speaker talking about his fight against his disease.

The helicopter pilot with the Factor V Leiden mutation also appealed her case, going all the way to the Army surgeon general to win a medical retirement.

But Miller, the Army ranger, did not fare so well. Even though he had the same disease as Platt, he lost his appeal and was discharged without benefits in 2005.

He still has to monitor his slow-growing tumors and be on the lookout for new ones. But without Tricare coverage, he can't afford to see a civilian doctor close to his home in Oak Ridge, Tenn.

Instead, he travels an hour and a half to the Veterans Affairs facility in Johnson City [Tennessee] at least twice a year. Every so often, he makes the three-hour drive to another VA facility in Lexington, Ky., to see a neurologist with expertise in his disease.

The worry never leaves him. His genes guarantee that he will never be cured.

> "[If] society should bear the cost [of genetic-related medical expenses], [and] if this generalizes, then each person would be obligated to pay the cost incurred by others because of bad luck."

Society Should Not Be Asked to Sacrifice for Those with Genetic Disorders

Fred E. Foldvary

In the following viewpoint, Fred E. Foldvary argues that extra expenses incurred by any genetic disorder should logically fall on those who accepted the risk by conceiving the child; hence, expectant parents should be required to obtain genetic medical insurance priced according to their known genetic factors. Foldvary is a professor of economics at Santa Clara University in California; senior editor of The Progress Report, *an independent daily news e-zine published by the Benjamin Banneker Center for Economic Justice; and the author of several books including* The Half-Life of Policy Rationales *and* The Soul of Liberty.

As you read, consider the following questions:

1. What does Foldvary list as some of the costs inherently assumed by all expectant parents?

Fred E. Foldvary, "Must We Subsidize Genetic Flaws?" *The Progress Report*, May 26, 2008. Reproduced by permission.

2. According to Foldvary, why is the Genetic Information Nondiscrimination Act unfair to the public at large?

3. How do insurers define "moral hazard"?

Nature sometimes plays tricks on us, and a baby is born with genetic flaws. That person can require huge medical expenses the rest of his life. Who should pay the cost?

The parents should bear the cost at least until the child becomes an adult. To avoid ruining their finances, they should be able to obtain insurance against their children being born with genetic flaws. The insurance would be more costly for parents who have known genetic conditions that could be passed on to their children, but parents would make a knowing choice about whether to incur these costs.

It could well be questioned why the person with genetic problems should bear the medical cost when he is an adult. It was not his choice to be born. It can also be questioned why society should bear the cost, since if this generalizes, then each person would be obligated to pay the cost incurred by others because of bad luck. No, logically the cost should be on the parents, and it should be covered by insurance.

The Risks Inherent in Conception

When parents decide to have a child, they know they are obligating themselves to pay many costs. They voluntarily take on themselves the cost of housing, feeding, and providing medical care for their offspring. If they create a child who will have medical costs because of genetic flaws, they as the creators should bear the costs, as they willingly took on the risk.

Policy should enforce this parental responsibility by requiring them to obtain genetic medical insurance before the child is born. This insurance would cover all medical costs, minus small co-payments, caused by genetic problems the child is born with. If the parents cannot afford the cost at that time, then it would be a lifetime liability not voidable by bankruptcy.

Insurance Against Birth Defects

[A new birth defect insurance policy,] offered through insurance giant ING, is the first of its kind in Australia, possibly the world, and is aimed at the growing number of older mothers. . . .

The risk for [having a baby with Down syndrome or another chromosomal abnormality] rises to one in 60 for 40-year-old women. . . .

The company would not require mothers to undergo genetic testing.

Louise Hall and Matthew Benns,
"Policy to Insure Against Birth Defects,"
Essential Baby, *April 27, 2008. www.essentialbaby.com.au.*

Governments often fail to do what is logical and efficient, so the U.S. federal government instead is now forcing the public to pay for genetic medical costs via higher insurance payments for everybody. In May 2008, the Genetic Information Nondiscrimination Act was enacted. It prohibits insurance firms from charging higher fees based on DNA tests showing that the insured customers are genetically predisposed to a disease.

Better to Insure People Against Genetic Problems Before Birth

People should not lose their medical insurance when genetic tests show they are at risk for illnesses. It is not their fault if they will have greater medical costs. Logically, they should be insured against genetic problems before they are born. That's what insurance is for—to avoid having to bear large costs because of circumstances beyond one's control.

There are now many tests one can take to discover genetic problems. But folks are afraid to take the tests when the results lead to higher medical insurance costs, or no insurance at all. The public benefits from this knowledge, and before-birth genetic insurance would join together personal and public benefits.

Severe genetic problems are rare, so the cost of before-birth genetic medical insurance would be small for most families, as the risk would be spread among the whole population. But for those parents with known genetic problems, the cost could be high, but why should they not bear the cost? By creating children likely to have large costs, they are imposing future social costs, and ethically those who create costs should bear them. If those parents don't have to pay those costs, it creates what insurers call "moral hazard," the imposition of greater social costs because people can make others pay the costs.

The medical impact of DNA testing will be a major 21st-century issue. DNA testing is becoming ever more widespread, so we should put genetic insurance on the table for discussion.

"Nearly 300 employees with developmental disabilities currently work at jobs they found through our career services. They are respected colleagues in law firms, retail, food service, government and elsewhere."

People with Genetic Disorders Can Become Productive Members of Society

Westchester County Business Journal

Westchester Arc, founded in 1949, is a United Way agency and a chapter of NYSARC. The agency, located in White Plains, New York, serves children, adults, and families dealing with developmental disabilities. The following selection describes the work of Westchester Arc and stresses its mission to achieve full respect and community inclusion for the disabled, who frequently function well in traditional schools and jobs as well as in self-advocacy. Anne M. Majsak, president of Westchester Arc, is also co-chair of its Parent Assistance Committee on Down Syndrome.

Westchester County Business Journal, "Building Independent Lives," vol. 45, March 6, 2006, pp. 2–5. Copyright Westfair Communications Inc. 2006. Reproduced by permission of Westchester Arc. www.westchesterarc.org.

As you read, consider the following questions:

1. What advertisement spurred the founding of Westchester Arc?

2. What is the name of Westchester Arc's program for the educational needs of young children?

3. Why did Westchester Arc adopt its current name?

"I own my own home, my own business, my own everything," declares Scott Fowler, a person with developmental disabilities. He was speaking to Westchester Arc staffers about "self-advocacy," people with disabilities making their own choices and speaking on their own behalf. It's a form of activism that's enriching the lives of individuals and the communities to which they increasingly contribute.

In 1949, a mother advertised to find playmates for her toddler with disabilities. The overwhelming response from similarly isolated families marked the founding of Westchester Arc, now the largest agency in the county [Westchester County, New York] serving children and adults with developmental disabilities. Our services include early intervention for newborns, pre-school, job placement, neighborhood residences and much more.

From the start, Westchester Arc has stood for community "inclusion" for the individuals we serve. Most of the youngsters affiliated with our Children's School for Early Development learn alongside typically developing classmates. Nearly half of them graduate to regular kindergarten classes in their home school districts. Children who were once non-verbal now speak in full sentences, sing songs and recite the alphabet.

Nearly 300 employees with developmental disabilities currently work at jobs they found through our career services. They are respected colleagues in law firms, retail, food service, government and elsewhere.

And they're good neighbors, living throughout the county in small, professionally supported homes. They may barbecue with the family next door, invite them over to watch a video, even bake a cake to welcome newcomers.

Over the decades, the expectations of people with developmental disabilities have risen as their accomplishments have grown. They are increasingly vocal about being viewed as individuals who vote, create art and fall in love.

Enhanced Mission

Westchester Arc's mission has evolved in response to these changing expectations. Once largely delivered in centralized settings, our services are now shaped to individual needs and mostly delivered in the community. "Life planning," at the heart of our philosophy, is a collaboration between self-advocates, families, educators and key social service professionals. The objective is to match interests and goals with milestones for achieving personal fulfillment.

At the same time, we have heard from self-advocates and their families that language, as a shaper of perception, must be more carefully attended to. The populations with whom we work are increasingly diverse in terms of diagnosis—including, but not limited to, autism, Down syndrome, cerebral palsy, mental retardation and epilepsy. The term "mental retardation," which has become stigmatized and does not describe, even in clinical terms, many of those we serve, is deeply disliked. Self-advocates wish to be treated as individuals having a wide range of abilities, not to be characterized by their disabilities. "Everyone has challenges of one sort or another," is an often-voiced observation.

To acknowledge these opinions, as well as the agency's evolving mission, we recently made a small, but significant, change to our name. [The original name was Westchester AHRC, from "Association for the Help of Retarded Children."] Westchester "Arc" symbolizes our effort to bridge gaps and

A Business Owner with Down Syndrome

[Tracey] Newhart, who has Down syndrome, was not allowed to graduate with her 2003 Falmouth High School classmates [or attend culinary arts college] because she failed the [Massachusetts Comprehensive Assessment System] test.... But she never let go of her culinary dreams.

[After four years of small baked-goods sales from home,] Newhart—now 25—began a triumphant new chapter in her life, as she swung open the doors to her own business, Tracey's Kitchen [on July 23, 2008].

Henry Rome, "Falmouth Woman Overcomes Challenges to Realize a Dream," Cape Cod Times, *July 24, 2008.*

build supportive connections between those we serve and their communities. It can no longer be misinterpreted as an acronym with negative associations.

Capital Campaign

Now Westchester Arc embarks on the most ambitious phase in its development as we raise funds for a "gateway to the community." Families have told us that our current facility, a former munitions factory in an industrial section of White Plains, projects a restrictive image, reinforcing traditional stereotypes about the people we serve. So we have mounted a capital campaign, the first in our history, to build a resource center that will be welcoming and provide flexible space consistent with the changing needs of people with developmental disabilities.

We envision conference rooms where people with disabilities and their families can network and meet social service professionals as they map out personal paths to community integration. We plan space to showcase accomplishments in the arts, to house conferences and advocacy events, to support training. We have already purchased land for this facility in Hawthorne, NY.

In addition, a Fund for the Future will be created to protect services that receive little or no financial support from the government. Our pre-school, guardianship and recreational services, for example, are heavily reliant on private donations. Our aim is to ensure that these and other innovative programs will be available to future generations of people with developmental disabilities.

Our fundraising goal for both the resource center and Fund for the Future is $7.5 million.

Encourage, Envision, Explore

We are currently in the drive's "quiet phase," a time to approach leading community members capable of making the generous contributions that will form a foundation for the campaign. We have already received significant support, notably a $2.2 million bequest from the estate of Gerard Gleeson [a longtime Westchester Arc supporter whose son was an active client]. . . .

Westchester Arc encourages individuals with developmental disabilities to "Envision Possibilities, Explore Choices," to break free from confining preconceptions and craft lives that are independent and fulfilling. We similarly ask the community at large to envision and explore the enrichment that results when all citizens have the opportunity to develop personal potential.

"People with disabilities have wants and desires just like you," says self-advocate Scott Fowler. "And like you, we are very capable of achieving them."

> "We have acknowledged the value of in-
> tegrated environments. What we don't
> countenance is a one-size-fits-all ap-
> proach that is relentlessly promoted by
> other interests in the disability-
> advocacy community."

Children with Disorders Need Special Education

Mark Richert

In the following viewpoint, Mark Richert discusses the problems inherent in a super-inclusive attitude that rejects any educational program designed solely for children with specific disabilities. While acknowledging the need for interaction with mainstream programs, he emphasizes the value of attention to individual needs and of programs carefully designed to meet the challenges inherent in certain disorders. Richert is director of the American Foundation for the Blind's Public Policy Center in Washington, DC, and an expert in disability-related civil rights issues.

As you read, consider the following questions:

1. What law requires "natural environments" for early childhood intervention services?

Mark Richert, "Nature that Won't Nurture," *Journal of Visual Impairment & Blindness*, vol. 101, September 2007, pp. 517–519.

2. According to Richert, what is "the most central aspect" of the law?

3. What does Richert consider the "most important task" in assuring every child will have the best education possible?

Imagine this scenario: A husband and wife, both blind, have twin daughters who are also visually impaired. While the girls were still toddlers, the parents decided to build on their own care and love for children and their own experiences with appropriate learning environments by founding a small community-based early childhood program for very young children with vision loss. The parents first got the idea to open such a program when a few other parents with kids who are blind asked if they could see how the twins played, the kinds of games or exercises that the parents did with them, or to simply let their children spend some time together with the twins. "Something magical happens when these precious little girls get to explore the wide world around them on relative terms of equality with friends who are like them," says the mother of the twin girls. "We wanted to share the joy we found in seeing what a difference the right environment can make for kids with as many families as possible." By the way, this scenario isn't completely hypothetical.

Dispensing with the Basic Questions

In evaluating this program, don't allow yourself to be unnecessarily sidetracked by nagging questions that can be dispensed with right away. Yes, this literally mom-and-pop program does rely on the expertise of professionals who know how to work with very young children with vision loss. Yes, the program meets all appropriate state and local requirements for operating such a center. No, the program doesn't exclude children with vision loss who may also have other disabilities. And, no, although the program tries to be innovative, it doesn't "experiment" on kids with techniques and approaches that aren't in the mainstream. The center, which has expanded to provide both early intervention and preschool services, receives high praise from every sector of consumer and professional communities both within and outside the field of vision loss. So, it would be safe to assume that everyone loves the program, right? Not on your life.

The Trouble with IDEA

For some time now, the federal special education law, the Individuals with Disabilities Education Act (IDEA), has required early childhood intervention services to be provided in so-called natural environments. Although the concept of a "natural environment" has never been adequately defined in regulations issued by the U.S. Department of Education, it is generally understood to mean that services must be provided in settings that also include children without disabilities. Yes, early intervention services can be provided in the home, but, generally speaking, services provided to children in center-based programs that are tailored to the needs of children with specific disabilities are not considered to be natural environments under IDEA. Yes, it is true that the law does make an exception to the overall mandate to provide services in natural environments. However, to justify a child's receipt of services at a center like the one described earlier, a successful argument must be made that appropriate services cannot be provided satisfactorily elsewhere. The question is, who gets to determine whether the services are appropriate or can be provided satisfactorily?

Pertinent Questions

The short, yet somewhat technical answer, is that the Individual Family Service Plan team (the group of parents and professionals and others who get together to set up a plan for the delivery of early intervention services for a child in accordance with IDEA) is supposed to make the determination that services can't be offered satisfactorily in the home or in other natural environments. However, if these teams meet at all, how frequently do you think they include professionals with training in the needs of blind or visually impaired infants and toddlers? How often do you think parents are fully aware of the range of possible services, let alone the places at which they are offered, that meet their child's needs? And, the most salient question of all, why must it be presupposed that an environment in which children with the same kind of disability play and learn together is somehow inferior to one in which services aren't tailor-made for them? In addition, why should it be necessary to go through an abstract exercise to justify placement in such a tailor-made setting as if there is something backward or unnatural about it?

The Resurgence of Inclusion

The very short answer to all these questions is ideology—otherwise known as inclusion—and it's nothing new. However, the inclusionists' emphasis on integration at the expense of specialized services is getting renewed attention. The Department of Education has recently proposed to better define the meaning of "natural environments," and the American Foundation for the Blind (AFB), along with many other organizations in the disability community, offered formal comment on this and other proposals relating to the Department of Education's intended regulations. Although the Department of Education doesn't have much choice but to at least echo what language exists in IDEA related to natural environments in the rules that it will ultimately publish, the department can, and often has, embellished provisions of IDEA through regulations that give fuller voice to ideological perspectives that Congress would not otherwise entertain.

An Extreme Perspective

If you don't believe that an extreme perspective about the meaning of natural environments is being urged on the Department of Education right now, you are mistaken. AFB's comments on the regulations asked the Department of Educa-

Support May Be Found in Camaraderie

For 14 years, Marlene and Arrie Belle Kinney dealt with the challenges of velo-cardio-facial syndrome (VCFS) [a genetic disorder that causes heart defects, oral dysfunction, and/or minor learning problems] without knowing another person going through the same thing.

Then last month, the mother and daughter traveled to Detroit for the 15th annual International Scientific Meeting on VCFS.... Arrie Belle for the first time bonded, sang and danced with other teens like her.

"It was fun to meet other kids that have gone through the same stuff," Arrie Belle said.

Alexis Garrobo,
"Teen Finds Support for Genetic Disorder,"
Island Packet, *August 5, 2008.*

tion to leave as much flexibility as possible in the definition of the term *natural environments*. However, not everyone shares our perspective. In fact, we have been told by some of the more outspoken advocates for children with developmental disabilities, for example, that they are urging the Department of Education to specifically limit the definition of natural environments to so-called "inclusive community" settings. There is absolutely no statutory basis for limiting the definition in this way, and this fact is acknowledged by our inclusionist friends. These advocates, nevertheless, see such an interpretation of natural environments that categorically excludes specialized settings as being in perfect harmony with the overall goals of the law—how incongruous, when the most central aspect of IDEA is the individuality of each child and the need for services that meet each child's needs. In AFB's comments to the Department of Education, we have acknowledged the value of integrated environments. What we don't countenance is a one-size-fits-all approach that is relentlessly promoted by other interests in the disability-advocacy community. Of course, we can fully understand the emotions that arise when children with disabilities, such as Down syndrome and mental retardation, are excluded from the education system because of the negative attitudes and discrimination they face every day. However, although some families and advocates may militantly believe that their children with disabilities are best served by participating in programs that are generically designed, these individuals can freely and forcefully advocate for their own children, while still leaving vital options open to the rest of us.

The Need for a Variety of Settings

Our field's most important task, then, is to be sure that the concept of natural environments is kept broad enough so that it includes a range of available settings that are free of bureaucratic and ideological roadblocks. AFB has taken the first step in trying to keep the Department of Education on track as it considers how to issue final regulations regarding natural environments. If the definition and application of natural environments in those rules does not reflect a balanced approach that recognizes the need for environments that truly nurture, our only option is to call upon Congress during the next review of IDEA to enact appropriate language for young children with vision loss. If, however, as is likely, the Department of Education fails to effectively clarify the meaning of the term *natural environments*, it will still be incumbent upon AFB and our partners to work with the Department of Education and our partners to ensure that parents know about the options that should be available and how to secure them for their children.

Finally, in regard to the center-based program described in the introduction of this comment, fewer and fewer children are being referred to centers for early intervention services under IDEA and, with all the other pressures being faced by nonprofit organizations these days, the long-term future of the program described in this piece, as well as other programs like it, is uncertain. What is certain, however, is that its future can and will be largely influenced by our field's willingness to speak up boldly about the need for both natural and nurturing environments for children who are visually impaired.

"With . . . early intervention and appropriate treatments, many students with autism can enter regular classrooms."

Children with Disorders Can Be Integrated into Mainstream School Districts

Joetta Sack-Min

While some researchers believe that certain types of autism are caused by genetics, debate continues on whether the disorder has a genetic basis. In the following viewpoint, Joetta Sack-Min looks at several New Jersey school districts that successfully educate large numbers of children with autism. While acknowledging the extra costs and frequent difficulties involved, the viewpoint argues that such children should be allowed and encouraged to learn alongside mainstream students to the greatest extent possible. Sack-Min also notes such options as including children without autism in special education classes, and the importance of working closely with parents. Sack-Min is associate editor of American School Board Journal, *a monthly periodical for school board members and school administrators, from which this selection is taken.*

As you read, consider the following questions:

1. According to Sack-Min, what is the cost range for educating a student with Autism in New Jersey's Brick Township?

2. What does one school administrator call "a great equalizer for all children"?

3. According to Sack-Min, what are some things that have "given students [with autism] a better chance to work or live independently"?

On its seaside perch, New Jersey's Brick Township beckons new residents with its small-town charm, Cape Cod–style homes, public beaches, and smattering of pizza joints—all within commuting distance to New York City.

School officials here, though, see families coming to the area for an entirely different reason: Their district, they say, has become a mecca for parents seeking a better education and therapies for their autistic children.

Brick's reputation for providing excellent education and services for children with autism is both flattering and vexing to the district. Educating children with this complex condition puts a strain on the budget and the staff—it costs between $20,000 and $43,000 annually to educate a child with autism in Brick.

"The cost is excessive, but we have an obligation to provide for all children in the community," says Melindo A. Perci, Brick's interim superintendent.

Diagnoses of autism in school-age children have soared 900 percent over the past decade—the fastest rising numbers of any childhood disability—and they show no signs of abating. While the reason for the increase is not clear, these numbers guarantee that most districts across the country are facing the challenge of educating autistic children.

Successful Education

Brick and several of its neighboring districts have found that students with all degrees of autism—those who are minimally affected and those who need intensive treatments—can have successful educational experiences. Their strategies include providing special preschool classes for students with autism, integrating the arts and music into their curriculum, and working closely with parents and parent groups.

"Just because they have autism doesn't mean they shouldn't have these opportunities," says Michael Dicken, principal of Bankbridge Development Center in Sewell, N.J.

Nationally, about one in 150 children are believed to have autism, a condition caused by abnormalities in the brain structure and function that occurs nearly four times more often in boys. The most obvious symptoms include unusual behaviors, communication and language difficulties, and socialization problems. Many autistic children also struggle with other physical conditions, including mental retardation. . . .

New Jersey school administrators are not concerned with statistics or the causes of autism. Each day they must confront the disorder with the best research and resources available, in hopes that with a good education and treatments these students will reach their maximum potential—whether that means entering a prestigious college or crossing the street without help.

Research-Based Curriculum

Treatment options and education methods abound for autism, and educators must balance the desires of parents wanting to use an untried treatment with what they know works.

Brick, for instance, never strays from its policy to use only research-based programs and strategies, says Julie Wolff, a behavioral analyst. The district's autism program is based on a curriculum that emphasizes verbal behavior and applied behavioral strategies, supported by research by famed psychologist B.F. Skinner.

In the early years, classes for students with autism have numerous aides who teach students individually. Often, classes with young children are divided into "centers" where an aide works with only one or two children at a time on a specific lesson.

For instance, in one elementary classroom in Brick, students with autism rotated between four centers that included activities such as reading and handwriting. Special education teacher Jennifer McDonald notes there was little interaction among the students, but they already had made progress in learning to greet and make eye contact with guests.

Because the students have different personalities and learn at dramatically different levels, McDonald creates individualized lessons for each child, keeps daily communication logs, and speaks with their parents at least three times a week. Each student also receives individualized speech and occupational therapies.

A Comprehensive Approach

[Brick's neighboring school district] Marlboro uses a more comprehensive curriculum that uses a multifaceted approach, including Skinner's verbal and behavioral techniques. Its Early Learning Center houses preschool classes for children with autism and other disabilities and all of the district's kindergarten classes.

Historically, New Jersey has not embraced inclusion as strongly as other states. While educators here say they support mainstreaming children with autism into their regular classes, some caution that a failed attempt at inclusion could have more severe ramifications for autistic students because of their social weaknesses.

Marlboro's programs to educate all but the most severely disabled autistic students within its schools not only provides significant savings in private tuition and transportation costs but also allows the district to place students in mainstream classes where appropriate.

"One thing that attracts parents to this district is that their children can go to regular classes," says Marlboro school board member Cynthia Green. "It's our goal to have a program that is comparable if not better than the private facilities."

At Marlboro's Early Learning Center, school officials carefully mainstream their preschool and kindergarten students with autism through strategies such as inclusive art and music classes, "reverse mainstreaming" that allows nondisabled students to come to the special education classes, and a preschool class with both autistic and nondisabled students who win seats through a lottery.

"Arts are a great equalizer for all children," says center principal Kathryn Arabia. Music classes, for instance, draw out the nonverbal autistic students.

The preschool programs also show that with the early intervention and appropriate, treatments, many students with autism can enter regular classrooms. Last year, 37 of the 55 preschool students with autism at the Early Learning Center moved into mainstream kindergarten classes.

Parents Are Part of the Plan

Parents of autistic children are, like many parents of children with disabilities, well-educated on their children's condition. Many are fierce advocates—making them forces to be reckoned with. Including and communicating with parents are important elements of Brick's autism program, as well as in Marlboro and [in] Gloucester [County, New Jersey, near Philadelphia].

Brick invites parents to its schools for guest lectures and meetings and works with the parents to explain why school officials have chosen a particular treatment plan, help them integrate the plan, and learn about other strategies that have been tried at home.

One of the Team

Megan Bomgaars, an Evergreen High School [Colorado] freshman with Down syndrome, joined the cheerleading squad last fall [2007].... Bomgaars, her teammates and coach ... are now being honored in the nation's capital [with a "National High School Spirit of Sport Award"].

Bomgaars' mother, Kris, hopes the entire cheerleading team, about a dozen girls, can attend the [July 2008] ceremony.

"They've changed her life," Kris Bomgaars said.

Nicole Vap, "Cheerleaders Closer to D.C. Trip,"
June 2008. www.9news.com.

"The more exposure parents have to sound information, the more it dispels some of the unrealistic expectations they may have," says Michael Zuccaro, a school social worker.

Parents in Marlboro have formed a committee that meets regularly with school administrators to discuss their children's education and other issues related to autism.

"It helps so much for parents who are concerned to come here and see the types of environments and meet people who understand," says Vicki Eisen, a mother of two children with autism and the co-president of the Special Children's Organization for Parents and Educators, which also serves as an informational and support group.

The Bankbridge school in Gloucester County has partnered with local businesses to build a parent resource center within the school. There, parents can browse books, magazines, or Web sites to learn more about their child's disability. As part of its parent involvement strategy, the school also hosts recreational programs for students on Friday nights.

Working with parents also saves significant funds by avoiding litigation, says Alan Ferraro, Brick's special education director.

"Once we had the program and the parents understood the program, the idea of litigation doesn't come up anymore," he says. "They're happy they see results, and they're supportive of what we do."

The Outlook Is Improving

As autism treatments become more effective, more students will be integrated into mainstream classes. For those on the severe end of the spectrum, who may have other disabilities, expectations and possibilities have grown dramatically in recent years, but these expectations also can pose the greatest challenges for schools.

Research and earlier interventions have given students a better chance to work or live independently. But many schools say they are still struggling to figure out the best education and course of treatments for secondary students with autism. Some experts say it's now time to find better strategies for transitions to the workplace or independent living.

"There's been a lot of energy placed on educating young children, but a lot of school districts struggle with not just young children," says Cathy Pratt, the director of the Indiana Resource Center for Autism at Indiana University. However, "the outcome data for students on the spectrum is not incredibly optimistic; too many individuals are unemployed or underemployed."

If an adolescent with autism is not capable of learning in regular academic classes by the time they enter high school, they are likely to focus primarily on vocational and life skills courses. Once students with disabilities "age out" of special education when they turn 21, they or their families are responsible for their well being.

Forging Partnerships

"The best thing we can do is educate the families and help point them to other resources and services," says Marlene Mc-Connell, president of the Gloucester Special Services School District board.

Brick has forged a partnership with a nursing home where students take on duties such as sorting silverware in the kitchen and delivering supplies. The district's lower-functioning students also take trips to the grocery store to learn how to shop. Even a recent excursion to a local IHOP restaurant became a learning experience: Each student was responsible for placing an order and paying the bill.

At the Bankbridge Development Center, the secondary education students have more obvious and severe disabilities than those in the preschool and elementary classes. Dicken estimates that about half of the students who enter the school in elementary grades will ultimately move back to their regular schools.

Integrated into the Larger World

Those who stay through their adolescent years spent most of their time in the wing that is primarily devoted to life skills. One large room has been set up as an apartment, with a small kitchen, laundry area, living room, bathroom, and bedroom. Students might bake cookies, clean the toilet, or watch cartoons. Another room has been set up as a makeshift convenience store, where students stock shelves and sort items.

"Even though it's a specialized environment, we want it to be normalized," Dicken says.

Some of Gloucester County's students now are working in local Wawa convenience stores and other stores and offices. One of the district's autistic graduates is now an aide in a Bankbridge preschool class. Dicken, for one, believes that the numbers of such success stories can only increase.

"The field is continually evolving," he says. "The dreams and hopes of the parents and the reality of the disability sometimes cross paths, but we will never sell a student short."

Periodical Bibliography

The following articles have been selected to supplement the diverse views presented in this chapter.

Anita L. Allen	"Genetic, and Moral, Enhancement," *Chronicle of Higher Education*, May 16, 2008.
Community Care	"Mum and Dad Must Let Go," February 22, 2007.
Madeline Drexler	"Your Genetic Test Is in the Mail," *Good Housekeeping*, May 2006.
Cathy Gulli	"A Demand for Down's," *Maclean's*, April 10, 2006.
Jesse J. Holland	"A Genetic 'Civil Rights Act' Passes Congress: Bush Expected to Sign Ban on Discrimination Based on DNA," *Houston Chronicle*, May 2, 2008.
Graham Hopkins	"The Scene Was Set for a TV Soap Episode," *Community Care*, November 8, 2007.
Paula Kluth, Douglas Biklen, Patricia English-Sand, and David Smukler	"Going Away to School," *Journal of Disability Policy Studies*, Summer 2007.
Lucy Phillips	"Ads Put Diversity in the Limelight," *People Management*, May 3, 2007.
Carol L. Russell	"How Are Your Person First Skills?" *Teaching Exceptional Children*, May/June 2008.
Aaron Notarianni Stephens	"Silent Echoes," *Exceptional Parent*, October 2008.
Keith Wiedenkeller	"Casting a Wider Net," *Film Journal International*, May 2007.

OPPOSING
VIEWPOINTS®
SERIES

CHAPTER 3

What Should Be Done to Address Genetic Disorders?

Chapter Preface

"Is perfection an entitlement?" asked columnist George Frederick Will in April 2005. Will, whose adult son has Down syndrome, was voicing a frustration common to many parents of children with genetic disorders: now that medical science can detect numerous disorders with fair accuracy in the early stages of fetal development, and large numbers of people are consequently opting to end their pregnancies rather than risk the hardships and suffering that may come with a disorder, those who choose to go ahead and have their babies often feel that the greater part of society despises them and their children.

"What is antiseptically called 'screening' for Down syndrome is, much more often than not, a search-and-destroy mission," wrote Will in another place. "As more is learned about genetic components of other abnormalities, search-and-destroy missions will multiply. . . . [Meanwhile, in the area of actually understanding how disabilities affect those who have them,] ignorance lingers. There are doctors who still falsely counsel parents that a Down syndrome person will never read, write or count change."

Adding to the issues surrounding fetal testing, genetic counseling and prebirth screenings can themselves give false results. Some people have had abortions on being told that the fetuses had disorders—when in fact the fetuses were healthy. Other parents have been assured through screening that their babies would be healthy—only to give birth to children with disorders.

"Wrongful-birth claims [lawsuits over doctors' failures to diagnose disorders which would have led parents to choose abortion] are on the rise," noted journalist Sabrina Rubin Erdely in 2005. "The more doctors are able to predict bad outcomes, the more they're being held responsible for accurately passing along that knowledge to patients." One woman had a child with Tay-Sachs disease—a disorder that means severe disability and death in early childhood—even though she had been screened and assured she did not carry the relevant gene; her doctor had misread a poorly written lab report. Erdely quotes this mother's reaction: "As a parent, you always want to protect your children.... Even if ... that means protecting your child from being born in the first place.... Does it hurt to say, 'Had I known, I wouldn't have had Evan?' Yeah. It does ... but I don't think anyone can truly understand what it's like to have a child and to know that child is going to do nothing but suffer for five years. To me, that's wrong, to knowingly put a child through that.'"

When, if ever, is abortion an appropriate method for preventing a genetic disorder? And can—or should—anything be done to reduce the number of children conceived with genetic disorders? This chapter explores such questions.

| "*Newborn screening saves lives and decreases disability.*"

Newborn Screening for Developmental Disabilities Can Be Beneficial

Bruce K. Lin and Alan R. Fleischman

Newborns are tested for many disorders, which, without treatment, can be very harmful or even deadly. Technological advances have expanded the list of disorders that can be identified by screening, which means more newborns can get the treatment that is needed to combat these disorders. The following viewpoint argues that instead of criticizing the inadequate distribution of funding for children's health programs, the focus should be on expanding the disorders that newborns are screened for and increasing the number of children who get the treatment they need. Bruce K. Lin is manager of public health initiatives and a contributor to the Hastings Center Report. *Alan R. Fleischman is senior vice president and medical director at the March of Dimes Foundation and a contributor to the* Hastings Center Report.

Bruce K. Lin and Alan R. Fleischman, "Screening and Caring for Children with Rare Disorders," *The Hastings Center Report*, vol. 38, May–June 2008, p. 3. Copyright © 2008 Hastings Center. Reproduced by permission.

As you read, consider the following questions:

1. How many disorders are recommended by a 2005 American College of Medical Genetics report to be included in the core panel for mandatory newborn screening?
2. What criteria were used to determine if a disorder should be included in the recommended panel of tests?
3. Why do critics argue that expert opinion is not enough to determine public health practice?

Newborn screening is a public health program that identifies genetic, metabolic, hormonal, and functional disorders in infants and provides comprehensive follow-up care. Without treatment, these disorders can result in devastating health consequences, and sometimes death. Newborn screening began in the mid-1960s, but has dramatically expanded in recent years. This is primarily due to new technology to reliably identify rare disorders, and to a 2005 report by the American College of Medical Genetics [ACMG], commissioned by the United States Health Resources and Services Administration, that recommended mandatory newborn screening for a core panel of twenty-nine disorders. This report moves toward a national uniform newborn screening panel for serious disorders that have effective preventive interventions and treatments. It was enthusiastically endorsed by the Secretary's Advisory Committee on Heritable Disorders and Genetic Diseases in Newborns and Children, the American Academy of Pediatrics, and the March of Dimes.

Criticism of Newborn Screening

[Some experts] criticize the process of decision making and the criteria for inclusion of disorders in the ACMG report and argue that resources spent on newborn screening might be better spent on other child health initiatives. The ACMG process for developing the recommended panel of tests was the

From the "Marrakech Declaration" on Newborn Screening in the Middle East

The international community has achieved important advances in infant survival and the reduction of neonatal mortality. As a consequence, in view of the United Nations' Convention on the Rights of the Child (1989), governments must now focus increased attention on assuring our children's optimal development and to put in place policies to ensure that tomorrow's adults are as free as possible from disability that will limit achieving their potential. This is facilitated by early screening for congenital genetic disorders that are responsible for major disability; if not treated early, the costs of treatment of preventable disability will be prohibitive for society and the lives of children and their families will be tragically and unnecessarily limited. Systematic newborn screening for these genetic disorders is, thus, a necessity for public health programs based on the resources available.

Marrakech Newborn Screening Conference,
"Marrakech Declaration," November 15, 2006.

creation of a multidisciplinary committee and solicitation of broad expert opinion. Its criteria for including a disorder were: identification of the disorder before symptoms occur through a sensitive, specific test performed shortly after birth; and demonstrated benefit of early detection, timely intervention, and efficacious treatment.

These criteria seem consistent with the ethics of mandatory newborn screening debated over the last forty years. Reasonable people may disagree on the definition of "demonstrated benefit" and "efficacious treatment," but the ACMG group took those concerns quite seriously. Since the report's release, forty-two states—acting on the judgments of advisory committees comprised of health experts and community members—have adopted screening panels that include at least twenty-one of the twenty-nine core disorders.

Critics argue that expert opinion is not enough to determine public health practice, and that only evidence-based data are sufficient to set screening standards. However, the threshold for evidence-based public health practice for screening for rare diseases is intrinsically different from evidence-based clinical practice, and from the approach applied to screening common chronic conditions like cancer or diabetes. The nature of rare disorders generally precludes randomized clinical trials to determine effectiveness of standard approaches to diagnosis and treatment. Case reports of successful interventions in small numbers of affected children may be all that is available to determine efficacy of treatment. Going forward, a national evaluation of newborn screening programs to further assess clinical effectiveness of population-based efforts is certainly warranted.

The Benefits of Newborn Screening

Newborn screening saves lives and decreases disability. The latest figures show that over four thousand children per year have a treatable metabolic or hormonal disorder, and another twelve thousand have a hearing deficit requiring intervention. Certainly many more children are born prematurely, or develop asthma or obesity, and all deserve adequate resources to prevent and treat these disorders. But it seems wrong to ask groups of children with known serious conditions to compete for resources that will determine their future health. Critics who argue that newborn screening may take resources away from other programs that might benefit more children tacitly accept the reprehensible behavior of state policy makers and condone injustice when they cite examples like a state's diversion of Medicaid funds from prenatal care or asthma prevention to support newborn screening. Rather than pitting one group of needy children against another, shouldn't we focus our criticism on the injustice caused by inadequate resources allocated to children's health in general?

Newborn screening is an established, effective program to identify children with rare diseases and refer them for needed treatment. Rather than criticize the approach that led to the widely accepted national screening panel, we should assure that other disorders with efficacious treatment are systematically added to it, and that all children who suffer from rare disorders—regardless of where they are born or whether they are insured—receive the comprehensive follow-up they need.

| "From the perspective of the 'disability critique,' prenatal testing is rarely, if ever, in the interests of the future child."

Prenatal Testing for Adult-Onset Conditions Is Not Beneficial

Bonnie Steinbock

In this viewpoint, Bonnie Steinbock argues that prenatal testing for potential genetic disorders cannot be justified on the grounds that it is better to prevent the birth of a child who might have such a problem, because it is virtually impossible to determine future quality of life or future medical advances. Dr. Steinbock is a professor of health policy and philosophy at the University at Albany (New York state); her other writings include Life Before Birth: The Moral and Legal Status of Embryos and Fetuses, *and she is co-editor of* Ethical Issues in Modern Medicine, *7th edition.*

As you read, consider the following questions:

1. According to Steinbock, what type of circumstance justi-fies prenatal testing for genetic disorders as being in the child's interest?

Bonnie Steinbock, "Prenatal Testing for Adult-Onset Conditions: Cui Bono?" *Reproductive BioMedicine Online*, vol. 15, supplement 2, December 2007, pp. 38–42. Reproduced by permission.

2. In a Canadian study involving Huntington's disease screening, how many couples requested prenatal testing and then changed their minds?

3. Who "argued that someone who knew that he or she was at risk for Huntington's disease had a moral obligation not to reproduce"?

One might think that the debate [over prenatal screening for genetic disorders] is between those who generally oppose abortion . . . and those who do not. The abortion debate turns largely, though not entirely, on the moral status of the fetus—an issue that is not going to be addressed here. However, at least some disability advocates do not base their opposition to prenatal testing on a general opposition to abortion. [Biology and ethics professor] Adrienne Asch supports abortion (or a woman's right to choose abortion) when the woman, for whatever reason, does not want to become a mother. She opposes abortion when the woman wants to become a mother, but does not want to be a mother to a child with certain characteristics, e.g. a disabling condition. This is sometimes called the 'any/particular' distinction because it distinguishes between an abortion of any child, and an abortion only of a particular child, or particular type of child. Asch believes that the desire to abort a wanted child, when it is discovered that the child likely will have a disability, stems either from ignorance about what it would be like to raise such a child, or discriminatory attitudes toward people with disabilities, or both. From the perspective of the 'disability critique', prenatal testing is rarely, if ever, in the interests of the future child.

Preparing in Advance

There is one exception, and that is when prenatal testing is done not in order to terminate the pregnancy, but rather to learn about any special needs due to the disability. For example, if spina bifida is discovered *in utero*, the doctors will probably want to do a Caesarean section, since the travails of normal labour might further damage the child's spine. A woman who would not consider aborting a fetus with spina bifida might, for this reason, want prenatal testing in order to have the safest type of delivery. In addition, some conditions can be treated surgically immediately after birth or even *in utero*. Prenatal testing might also help the parents be better prepared to care for and raise a child with special needs.

Could this rationale for prenatal testing have implications for adult-onset conditions? Obviously, adult-onset conditions would not affect planning for the birth or medical care or education during childhood. However, it is possible that there are preventive measures that could be adopted during childhood to lessen the risk of developing an adult-onset disease. Perhaps a child at high risk for developing heart disease or diabetes as an adult might be able to reduce that risk with dietary modifications from childhood on, just as children born with phenylketonuria can avoid mental retardation with a severely limited diet. In such cases, prenatal genetic testing might have a benefit for the future child.

Genetic Predictions Are Far from Perfect

However, this justification for prenatal testing is dubious for two reasons. First, for most people and most adult-onset diseases, genetic testing is not predictive. . . . In diseases like heart disease and diabetes, the environment plays a large role in whether the individual develops the disease, even in the presence of genetic risk factors. For most adult-onset diseases, even if there are childhood interventions that could be taken, a prenatal genetic test will not reveal if the interventions are necessary or desirable. It should be remembered that interventions to prevent disease may themselves have adverse effects. (Sadly, this is also true for phenylketonuria [a genetic disorder where the body cannot utilize the amino acid phenylalanine], where a false positive could mean that a child was placed on a severely restrictive diet needlessly. Sometimes this has even resulted in brain damage to the developing infant brain, resulting ironically in mental retardation.)

The Most Predictive Genes

There are some adult-onset diseases where a small percentage of people inherit particular mutations that cause a strong predisposition to the disease in virtually any environment, making the tests highly (if not absolutely) predictive. For example, a very small percentage of women who get breast or ovarian cancer (about 1%) have the *BRCA1* or *BRCA2* gene variant. This means that they are born with a strong genetic predisposition to the disease. Women who have the *BRCA1* or *BRCA2* gene variant have up to an 85% risk of developing breast cancer by age 70, as compared with a 12% risk over a 90-year life span for women who do not have these mutations. Women who have the *BRCA1* or *BRCA2* gene variants could be identified prenatally. . . . The question is, what would be the point of prenatal testing for breast cancer? Certainly not to institute preventive measures in childhood. The only preventive measure is frequent screening in adulthood, or having the breasts and ovaries prophylactically removed. One need not do a prenatal test, or testing in childhood, to do this sort of prevention. The only reason for prenatal screening for breast cancer is to avoid the birth of a girl who is likely to have breast cancer at some point in her life. . . .

Declining the Huntington's Disease Test

If a genetic test had very strong predictive value, that is, if the test could reveal with near certainty that the individual would develop the disease, that might be a reason for wanting the test prenatally. An example is Huntington's disease (HD), an autosomal dominant adult-onset disease with virtually 100% penetrance. HD is a fatal and degenerative brain disorder.

Symptoms usually appear between the ages of 30 and 50; there is no cure and no treatment. It is possible to determine if a fetus carries the gene for HD by amniocentesis or chorionic villus sampling. If the prospective parents would terminate the pregnancy if the fetus were affected, they most likely would want the test. If they would not abort, there is no reason to have the test. Thus, the rationale for prenatal testing for HD depends on the willingness to abort. This has been borne out by a study in Canada, where prenatal genetic testing for HD has been available since 1986. Early survey data suggested that 32 to 65% of those couples with one partner at risk of developing HD would want prenatal testing. However, during the study, researchers found that only 14 couples (30%) initially requested prenatal testing, and of those 14, seven withdrew. (Admittedly, this is not a large sample.) 'The most frequently cited reason for declining prenatal testing was the hope that a cure would be found in time for their children.' This suggests that even where a test is strongly predictive of a dreadful disease, a significant number of people would decline the test, because they retain the hope that advances in medicine will prevent their child from getting the disease.

When Serious Problems Are Unavoidable

What if there was no hope of avoiding the disease? In such a case might abortion be viewed as being chosen (perhaps required) for the sake of the child? This idea is sometimes expressed when people say things like: 'It would be unfair to the child to be born in such a condition. If you knew your child would have condition X, how could you do that to a child?'. The condition might be a medical condition, but could also be a social condition, such as being born to an older father, who was unlikely to live to the child's adulthood, being born in extreme poverty, etc. This issue has been the subject of substantial literature. Some have taken the position that coming into existence can never be a harm to the individual, that life

Do You Really Need to Know?

Does a child, or her parent, need to know she carries the gene that makes her susceptible to breast cancer?

A "core piece of advice is you shouldn't do genetic testing just because it's available," said Dr. Douglas Diekema, who works on pediatric bioethics at Seattle Children's Hospital and Regional Medical Center. [He suggests asking yourself:] "If there is a test (that) came back positive, what would be the benefit for my child? Is there something we could do?"

Paul Nyhan, Seattle Post-Intelligencer, *July 29, 2008.*

is always worth living, whatever the magnitude of the disability or the amount of suffering. This seems far too strong. It is not difficult to imagine a life so brief and so filled with unrelievable suffering and so absent of the things that make life worth living that existence itself is not a benefit but a harm. A less extreme view holds that existence is a benefit except where the individual himself or herself, or a proxy acting on his or her behalf, would prefer non-existence. However, there is an ambiguity in the phrase 'preferring non-existence'. It could mean 'preferring never to have existed' or it could mean 'preferring to die', that is, not to go on living. There are notorious difficulties about ascribing preferences to infants and young children, which led [the late political and social philosopher] Joel Feinberg to use the device of a proxy chooser who, acting on behalf of the child, is rationally required to prefer never having come into existence to existence under the terrible and unavoidable conditions of the child's life. However, [bioethicist] John Robertson appears to take the other interpretation of the wrongful life test. He acknowledges that it is possible (though doubtful in reality) for there to be a case of wrongful life. The test he uses is 'where from the perspective of the child, viewed solely in light of his interests as he is then situated, any life at all with the conditions of his birth would be so harmful to him that from his perspective he would prefer not to live'. This is known as the wrongful life standard, after legal cases in which it was alleged that an infant plaintiff was harmed by being born, and owed damages by the negligent physician responsible for the child's birth, even though the physician did nothing either to cause the harmful condition or to prevent its occurrence. The only way to have avoided the child being born in such a condition would have been to avoid the child's birth altogether.

Wrongful Life Is Extremely Rare

The wrongful life condition can explain how the child has been harmed and wronged. If the child's life is so terrible that the child himself or herself would prefer nonexistence, then the child would be better off unborn. Being brought into existence under such conditions both harms and wrongs the child. The difficulty with this standard is that it is hardly ever met. Most disabilities, even very severe ones, do not impose terrible suffering. Indeed, some of the most devastating conditions, such as anencephaly, impose no suffering, as it seems likely that the child experiences nothing, and therefore is not in pain. In addition, many people who have serious disabilities report having lives well worth living. They do not wish that they were dead or that they had never been born. It becomes, then, a real challenge to explain how children can be said ever to have been harmed or wronged by birth with a serious disability, or to explain the basis of the alleged obligation to prevent their births. It may be that, in many cases, the correct explanation for the obligation to avoid procreation stems from impersonal, rather than person-affecting, reasons. . . .

Morally Obligated Not to Reproduce?

If it is difficult to explain the obligation not to have a child with a seriously disabling condition, the difficulty is compounded in the case of adult-onset diseases. Consider one of the worst, HD. Before the test for HD was developed, individuals could know of their risk only if either of their parents had HD. If they had inherited the gene, every child they had would have a 50% chance of inheriting the disease as well. But this could not be known until they became symptomatic, usually not until their late 40s or 50s—long after reproductive age for most people. In 1978, [humanities professor] Laura Purdy argued that someone who knew that he or she was not at risk for HD had a moral obligation not to reproduce. Had Arlo Guthrie taken her advice, he would not have had his three children. As it turned out, he had not inherited the HD gene from his father, Woody Guthrie. His gamble paid off. Today, with predictive genetic testing available, there need be no gamble. Anyone at risk can be tested for the HD gene, prior to reproducing. If the test is negative, the individual need not worry about passing on the disease. But what if the test is positive? Is it clear that there is a moral obligation not to reproduce? Arlo Guthrie allegedly felt that even if he passed on the gene, it would not be wrong of him to have children. He felt that he had had a good life, and did not wish that he had not been born. Therefore, he would not feel guilty providing his children with 40 or 50 years of disease-free life, even if they developed HD. Moreover, as mentioned above, some of those at risk for HD do not wish to avoid reproduction, because they hope that a cure will be found in the children's lifetimes. The same argument applies more strongly to breast cancer, which has less penetrance and where prophylactic measures are possible.

A Life Worth Living

What about schizophrenia? On the one hand, it is likely to occur much earlier, reducing the amount of 'good time' before the onset of disease. On the other hand, people do manage to live with schizophrenia, and many are able to control their symptoms with medication. Given that genetic tests cannot reveal how severe the disease will be, it is difficult to maintain that there is an obligation to undergo prenatal testing where there is a family history of the disease, or that reproduction must be avoided 'for the sake of the child'. Whether parents might justifiably wish to avoid having a child at high risk for schizophrenia is a separate question.

Prenatal genetic testing is usually desired on grounds of reproductive autonomy. It is the author's view that individuals who want to avoid the birth of a child with a severe disability are morally entitled to do so by having an abortion, though that claim has not been defended here. At the same time, it is much more difficult to justify prenatal testing and selective abortion as being for the sake of the child who otherwise would have been born, because in almost all cases the child, once born, will have a life worth living. This is so even in the case of severe disability at birth, and much more so in the case of adult-onset disorders.

> *"The availability of tests [for genetic disorders] earlier in pregnancy mean[s] that if [people] opt for an abortion it can be safer and less public."*

Aborting a Fetus with a Genetic Disorder Is a Personal Decision

Amy Harmon

In the following selection, Amy Harmon presents the viewpoints of several people, some of whom describe themselves as generally pro-life, who had aborted pregnancies after learning their children would have genetic disorders. Recent improvements in the safety and reliability of prenatal testing have made early abortion a more feasible option but have also increased the number of prospective parents who have to make difficult and heart-wrenching decisions. Harmon is a national correspondent for the New York Times, *specializing in the impacts of science on everyday life. Her article series on genetic technology, "The DNA Age," won a 2008 Pulitzer Prize.*

As you read, consider the following questions:

1. Testing for what genetic disorder was recommended in all pregnancies with a Caucasian parent in fall 2001?
2. According to Harmon, what are "perhaps the hardest cases for both doctors and patients"?
3. What is the name of one support group for those who chose abortion because of fetal health problems?

Lying in the darkened doctor's office, Kate Hoffman stared at the image of the 11-week-old fetus inside her on the ultrasound screen, a tiny ghost with a big head. It would have been so sweet, Ms. Hoffman said, if something had not been so clearly wrong.

Ms. Hoffman's first three children had been healthy, and she was sure this one would be, too. She was not planning to have the amniocentesis procedure often used to test for fetal health problems, preferring to avoid even the slightest risk that the insertion of a needle into her uterus would cause her to miscarry.

But when her doctor told her there was a new way to assess the chance of certain abnormalities with no risk of miscarriage—a blood test and special sonogram—she happily made an appointment.

The result, signaling that the child had a high chance of having Down syndrome, thrust Ms. Hoffman and her husband into a growing group of prospective parents who have learned far more about the health of their fetus than was possible even three years ago [2001].

Better Tests, Hard Choices

Fetal genetic tests are now routinely used to diagnose diseases as well known as cystic fibrosis and as obscure as fragile X, a form of mental retardation. High-resolution sonograms can detect life-threatening defects like brain cysts as well as treatable conditions like a small hole in the heart or a cleft palate sooner and more reliably than previous generations of the technology. And the risk of Down syndrome, one of the most common birth defects, can be assessed in the first trimester rather than waiting for a second-trimester blood test or amniocentesis.

Most couples say they are both profoundly grateful for the new information and hugely burdened by the choices it forces them to make. The availability of tests earlier in pregnancy mean that if they opt for an abortion it can be safer and less public.

But first they must decide: What defect, if any, is reason enough to end a pregnancy that was very much wanted? Shortened limbs that could be partly treated with growth hormones? What about a life expectancy of only a few months? What about 30 years? Or a 20 percent chance of mental retardation?

"I Don't Look at It as an Abortion"

Striving to be neutral, doctors and genetic counselors flood patients with scientific data, leaving them alone for the hard conversations about the ethics of abortion, and how having a child with a particular disease or disability would affect them and their families. There are few traditions to turn to, and rarely anyone around who has confronted a similar dilemma.

Against the backdrop of a bitter national divide on abortion, couples are devising their own very private scales for weighing whether to continue their pregnancies. Often, political or religious beliefs end up being put aside, trumped by personal feelings. And even many of those who have no doubts about their decision to terminate say the grief is lasting.

"It was never even anything I had considered until I had the bad results," said Ms. Hoffman, who ended her pregnancy last year after a follow-up test confirmed that her child, if it survived, would have Down syndrome. "It was the hardest decision I ever had to make."

She and her husband, Drew, of Marblehead, Mass., decided that the quality of the child's life, and that of the rest of their family, would be too severely compromised. "I don't look at it as though I had an abortion, even though that is technically what it is," she added. "There's a difference. I wanted this baby."

Judgments from All Sides

Whatever they choose, couples find themselves exposed to judgments from all sides. Several of those interviewed asked that personal details be withheld because they had let friends and family believe that their abortion was a miscarriage. Others say they have been surprised that even conservative parents, who never faced such decisions themselves, have counseled them to abort rather than face too hard a life. . . .

Amy D., a preschool teacher in Livingston, N.J., who terminated a pregnancy after finding out the child would have cystic fibrosis, remembers falling to her knees in the schoolyard when her genetic counselor called her with the test results.

She and her husband did not know what cystic fibrosis was and had no known family history of the disease, which causes progressive lung failure and carries an average life expectancy of 35 years. But in the fall of 2001, the American College of Obstetricians and Gynecologists recommended that a blood test for the gene mutations that cause the disease be offered in all pregnancies when either the man or woman is Caucasian.

What Might Have Been

Amy D. screened positive as a carrier in August 2002, shortly after she found out she was pregnant with her first child.

A Matter of Individual Judgment

Pregnant women and couples are the only ones in a position to evaluate what is in the best interest of themselves and their potential child. The most loving and responsible women and couples will consider all options and circumstances and make the wisest choice for themselves, and their family. Society cannot compel people to forfeit their own rights (or life) to save the life of another. Such a sacrifice must be entirely voluntary.

Abortion Rights Coalition of Canada, "Position Paper #25: Abortions for Genetic Reasons," February 2006.

When her husband also turned out to be a carrier, there was a one-in-four chance that their fetus would have the disease. An amniocentesis showed that it would. Having watched her husband shrink from scenes of suffering, whether in movies or during his own father's illness, she said she knew her marriage would not survive having a severely ill child. "My life would have been caring for my child, which would have been fine if she would be O.K," said Amy D., who asked that her last name be withheld for fear that anti-abortion activists would harass her. "But she wasn't going to be O.K."

After months of depression, she said she is thrilled to be adopting an infant boy from Asia. Still, when she watches the 20-something woman with cystic fibrosis on MTV's "Real World" dating and getting body piercings, Amy D. says she cannot help wondering if her daughter, who would have been named Sydney Frances, would have been like that—at least for a while. . . .

The Hardest Cases

Perhaps the hardest cases for both doctors and patients come when technology provides enough information to raise concerns about the health of a fetus but not enough to make a conclusive diagnosis. When Tom Horan and his wife learned in April that their fetus's legs were bowed and shortened, they were told that the condition could be healed through braces, growth hormones and surgical procedures in childhood.

But before they decided what to do, a closer examination by a specialist with a 3-D ultrasound machine revealed other deformities: the left arm was missing below the elbow, and the right hand was only partially developed. Moreover, sometimes such features are a sign of a neurological impairment, the doctors told them, but in this case it was impossible to tell.

"Our main concern was the quality of life that the child would have growing up with such extensive limb deformities, even in the absence of cognitive problems," Mr. Horan said. He and his wife, who have three other children, were reared Roman Catholic and had never considered terminating a pregnancy. Yet even his father, Mr. Horan said, who had long been opposed to abortion, supported their decision to end the pregnancy.

"Not Just a Questions of Right and Wrong"

"Confronted with this question and knowing what we knew, it changed his mind," Mr. Horan said. "It's not just a question of right and wrong; it introduces all sorts of other questions that one has to consider, whether it is the survivability of the child, quality of life of parents, quality of life of siblings, social needs. And it becomes much more real when you're confronted with an actual situation."

After the termination, an examination showed that if he survived, Mr. Horan's son would have had an extremely rare condition, Cornelia de Lange syndrome. He would have been severely mentally and physically disabled.

The news was a relief to Mr. Horan, who said he felt sadness and grief, but no regrets about the decision. But before the diagnosis, he said, he felt guilt and uncertainty. At 21 weeks, the fetus was not viable when his wife underwent induced labor and delivery but survived briefly.

"Our son lived for three hours, and I spent almost all that time holding him," Mr. Horan said. "I worried that I had decided to rob him of his life simply based on limb deformities. I wondered about the ethical implications of taking a life simply on that basis. What did that say about me?"

Contradicting Beliefs

That is just one of many questions that couples ask themselves as they confront the ethics of whether to abort a fetus with disabilities. But because it is such a charged subject, many are loath to discuss it with others. They say there is often no outlet for their grief.

"I cannot turn on the computer any day without getting an e-mail from someone who needs help," said the woman who runs A Heartbreaking Choice, an Internet support group for people who have terminated pregnancies because of their fetus's health. "But nobody's talking about it. Certainly not here in southeastern Virginia," where anti-abortion groups are so vocal.

A nurse practitioner in New Jersey said her parents, in-laws and best friends all believed she had a miscarriage. In reality, after having an amniocentesis because she was 39, she discovered that the male fetus had two X chromosomes in addition to a Y chromosome. Men with the condition, Klinefelter's syndrome, have little body hair and feminine features. Some lead normal lives, but others have learning difficulties and virtually all are sterile.

"We didn't want to put ourselves in the position to be judged, because it was difficult enough as it was," she said, though she said she wished she had told her family about the diagnosis. "I was thinking about Klinefelter's constantly, but I couldn't mention it to anyone."

Dr. John Larsen, chairman of the department of obstetrics and gynecology at George Washington University Medical Center, said the sense of taboo was amplified by how often people's choices contradict their previously held beliefs.

"People will come into my office in tears and say they've been against abortion their whole lives," he said, "but they'll make an exception for themselves."

"We cherish our friends and family members and think their unexpected extra chromosome is not the most important thing about them."

It Is Not Acceptable to Abort Fetuses Showing Down Syndrome

Patricia E. Bauer

In the following viewpoint, journalist Patricia E. Bauer criticizes the trend toward testing every pregnancy for Down syndrome and aborting whenever the test comes back positive. People with Down syndrome are not "bad outcomes," she argues, and it is time a comprehensive study was made of their quality of life. Bauer is former senior editor of the Los Angeles Times Sunday Magazine; *former reporter, bureau chief, and special assistant to the publisher of* The Washington Post; *and mother of a young woman with Down syndrome.*

As you read, consider the following questions:

1. How many living U.S. citizens have Down syndrome?

2. What was awarded to a Florida couple who sued their doctor for failing "to detect an obscure genetic condition prenatally"?

3. Whom does Bauer refer to as "the real experts" on Down syndrome?

All across the land this fall [2007], people have been gathering to promote awareness and acceptance of Down syndrome. Central to their message is the idea that people with the condition are valued family members who lead happy, fulfilling lives.

At the National Institutes of Health and the Centers for Disease Control and Prevention, scientists have been meeting to develop research agendas to improve the lives of people with Down syndrome, the genetic condition that results when a person has three copies of the 21st chromosome instead of the usual pair.

But in the places where medicine is practiced, a very different and less benevolent awareness of Down syndrome reigns. As a result of recent changes in technology and standards of care, women are undergoing prenatal diagnostics for Down syndrome in unprecedented numbers—often multiple times during their pregnancies. When the condition's detected, they are having abortions at rates that are thought to approach 90 percent.

Those of us who actually have relationships with people with Down syndrome, and who see them achieving and thriving in their communities, view this paradox as baffling at best, tragic at worst.

Not Something to Be Shunned at All Cost

We cherish our friends and family members and think their unexpected extra chromosome is not the most important thing about them. And we worry that the relentlessness of genetic testing is amplifying stigma and bias against the 350,000

Down Syndrome as a Part of a Person's Identity

Asking whether I am at risk for having another child with Down syndrome is akin to asking whether I am at risk for having another child with brown hair, gorgeous green eyes, her father's hand-eye coordination, or her mother's love for books. It implies that Down syndrome is something separate from Penny, something that could be extracted if only we had the proper tools and procedures. But that extra chromosome is intrinsic to Penny's being. To take away Down syndrome is to take away Penny.

Amy Julia Becker,
"Down Syndrome Is a Part of Who My Daughter Is,"
The Philadelphia Inquirer, *July 20, 2008.*

flesh-and-blood Americans who have the condition, as well as people who have other conditions that are now or soon will be prenatally discoverable.

In recent conversations with obstetricians and gynecologists, I've found that we family members aren't the only ones with these fears. Physicians say they're disturbed by mounting demands from prospective parents for nothing less than the "perfect" child, and by lawyers who troll for lawsuits against doctors who have the misfortune to deliver nonstandard babies. Not long ago, a Florida jury awarded a couple more than $21 million when their doctor failed to detect an obscure genetic condition prenatally.

Doctors are left to practice defensive medicine, ordering expensive tests and drowning patients in mind-numbing data, while parents labor under the misapprehension that they have a duty to terminate if the tests so dictate.

It Might, It Might Not

It's bad enough that the prenatal screens themselves aren't exact. They can't tell for sure whether a fetus has an extra chromosome, only the Las Vegas odds that it might. (For more certainty, wait a while and have another test.) They have significant rates of both false positives and false negatives, which is the medical way of saying they're not infrequently wrong. It's no wonder pregnant women are stressed.

And here's the worst part: The diagnostics carry the unspoken message that people with Down syndrome are "bad outcomes," people whose lives are not worth living. Yet there hasn't been a comprehensive effort to collect data on the outcomes of adults with the condition, nor have there been well-funded efforts to develop treatments for them.

Nobody thinks the tests are going away. Still, there is much physicians could do to reform the testing process, reducing women's stress and lessening the risk of stigma against people with Down syndrome and other genetic differences.

Doctors should encourage couples to explore their beliefs about when life begins, and the value of people with disabilities, before asking about screening. Couples need to know that a conversation about screening may well wind up a conversation about abortion. Is that somewhere they want to go?

The Risks and Benefits of Testing

Doctors should make clear the risks, benefits and limitations of the tests before asking couples if they wish to screen. Couples should be told that the tests are voluntary and that their purpose is not to offer reassurance (as some doctors say) but rather to identify genetic and developmental differences in fetuses.

Doctors should provide accurate, current information about Down syndrome to couples in a respectful context before asking if they wish to screen, while people are calm and can absorb information. These discussions should be conducted in people-first language: "child with Down syndrome," not "Down's child." Outdated words to avoid: "Mongolism" and "Mongoloid."

Doctors should support and respect every woman's right to choose whether to be screened and whether to continue a pregnancy. Once women have made their decision, they should not be badgered to revisit the question.

Doctors delivering an unexpected diagnosis should refer parents to the real experts—other parents—through local support groups and should also provide resources from national Down syndrome organizations.

Accumulating Reliable Information

Most important, physicians should insist on comprehensive research into the quality of life and outcomes of people with Down syndrome and their families, and those data should be used to develop accurate materials to share with prospective parents.

After all, if physicians don't have reliable information about the lives of people with Down syndrome, how can they advise patients? And how can patients possibly give informed consent?

In the meantime, I'll keep hoping for acceptance of genetic diversity. That would be the best resolution of all.

> "One woman related that after her baby
> was born, 'the doctor flat out told my
> husband that this could have been pre-
> vented ... at an earlier stage.'"

Prenatal Testing for Genetic Disorders Dehumanizes All Who Have Disorders

Ramesh Ponnuru

In the following viewpoint, Ramesh Ponnuru argues that prenatal testing for genetic disorders expresses and encourages a long-standing—though now rarely openly admitted—attitude that an "imperfect" person is unfit to live. The same idea fueled the "eugenics" that, in the early twentieth century, promoted forced sterilization to head off the birth of "imbeciles" and "morons." Ponnuru, a senior editor for National Review, *has published columns and articles in a number of prominent periodicals including* Time, The Wall Street Journal, *and the* New York Times. *This selection first appeared in his book* Party of Death.

Ramesh Ponnuru, "Weeding Out the Unfit," *The Human Life Review*, vol. 32, Spring 2006, p. 29+. Copyright © 2006 Human Life Foundation, Incorporated. Reproduced by permission.

As you read, consider the following questions:

1. According to Ponnuru, do more or fewer people favor abortion to prevent genetic disorders, than favor abortion in general?

2. What prominent historical figure "condemned eighty-five million Americans as 'mediocre to imbecile'"?

3. In 1982, an infant with Down syndrome died after his parents refused lifesaving surgery; by what name did that event come to be known?

In recent years, many Americans have become concerned that our schools "overtest" children. In truth, however, the first test to which they are subject comes long before school, and it's the highest-stakes test of all. We test our children in the womb and, depending on the results, decide whether they live or die.

The number of children in this country with Down syndrome, for example, has fallen over the last fifteen years. That's not because a cure has yet been found. The rising number of older women having babies should, indeed, have increased the prevalence of the syndrome. The reason for the drop is the increased use of "second-trimester screening." When people find out that they are having a child likely to have the syndrome, more than 80 percent of them opt to abort the baby. Prenatal testing is routine, and its point is less to prepare parents for the challenges of raising a disabled child, or to determine whether the baby needs medical treatment in the womb, than to determine whether to kill the baby. We abort most children with Down syndrome, or Tay-Sachs disease, or spina bifida, or cystic fibrosis. And we abort some children who don't have those conditions because the tests aren't foolproof.

Nasty Expectations

Parents of children with Down syndrome often report that they were encouraged to have an abortion or, what might be worse, simply expected to have one. (Just as parents are simply expected to have prenatal testing, even when that testing poses risks to the baby. Physicians who don't offer the tests might later find themselves facing a "wrongful birth" lawsuit—a kind of legal action that itself reflects the influence of abortion on our mores.) [Disability rights spokesperson] Beth Allard reported that an obstetrician had told her that her child might have the syndrome [he did—she had him anyway], and then explained what that meant. "It could just be hanging off of you, drooling," the doctor said, and then "contort[ed] her face into a saggy, expressionless imitation of what a child [with the syndrome] might look like."

A study released in 2005 found that a majority of mothers of children with Down syndrome reported that their doctors accentuated the negative, that many got out-of-date information about the trials of living with the condition, and that pressure to have an abortion was not uncommon.

Criticized for a Humane Decision

Parents also sometimes report that their decision *not* to abort elicits criticism, even from strangers. One woman related that after her baby was born, "the doctor flat out told my husband that this could have been prevented . . . at an earlier stage." [Journalist and disability-rights advocate] Patricia Bauer wrote an op-ed about the phenomenon. "I see the way people look at [my daughter]: curious, surprised, sometimes wary, occasionally disapproving or alarmed."

> At a dinner party not long ago, I was seated next to the director of an Ivy League ethics program. In answer to another guest's question, he said he believes that prospective parents have a moral obligation to undergo prenatal testing and to terminate their pregnancy to avoid bringing forth a child with a disability, because it was immoral to subject a child to the kind of suffering he or she would have to endure. (When I started to pipe up about our family's experience, he smiled politely and turned to the lady on his left.)

Margaret does not view her life as unremitting human suffering (although she is angry that I haven't bought her an iPod). She's consumed with more important things, like the performance of the Boston Red Sox in the playoffs and the dance she's going to this weekend. Oh sure, she wishes she could learn faster and had better math skills. So do I. But it doesn't ruin our day, much less our lives. It's the negative social attitudes that cause us to suffer.

Bauer's op-ed drew several letters decrying her as "sanctimonious."

Public Attitudes

Senators Sam Brownback and Ted Kennedy, a pro-life Republican and a famously pro-choice Democrat, are co-sponsoring a bill to provide funding so that doctors can provide parents with better information, including contact information for support groups for parents of children with congenital diseases or syndromes. It's a worthy effort.

But the testimony of parents such as Bauer suggests that our country now has a reasonably strong social norm that disabled babies should be aborted. This type of diversity we do not wish to tolerate. . . . Americans are much less supportive of abortion than is commonly thought. But no such claim can be made about abortion of the disabled. In every poll, Americans strongly support the right to abort *them*. [Bioethicist] Leon Kass, who has thought deeply about medical ethics for years, concludes, "We are largely unaware that we have, as a society, already embraced the eugenic principle, 'Defectives shall not be born,' because our practices are decentralized and because they operate not by coercion but by private reproductive choice." We are, however, occasionally given glimpses of the import of our choices.

The Alleged Public Health Benefits of Legal Abortion

When Joycelyn Elders was Governor Bill Clinton's surgeon general in Arkansas, she testified before Congress in favor of the Freedom of Choice Act. Abortion "has had an important and positive public-health impact," she said. It "has reduced the number of children afflicted with severe defects." She gave an example: "The number of Down's [sic] syndrome infants in Washington state in 1976 was 64 percent lower than it would have been without legal abortion." The remark did not keep her from being nominated by Clinton, a few years later [when he was president], to be the surgeon general of the United States, or from being confirmed.

We like to think that eugenics is a thing of the past, that it died in the ashes of Nazi Germany. Today's Supreme Court would not bless a forced sterilization with the words [on Oliver Wendell Holmes's opinion in the 1927 Supreme Court case *Buck v. Bell*], "Three generations of imbeciles are enough." (Also: "It is better for all the world, if instead of waiting to execute degenerate offspring for crime, or to let them starve for their imbecility, society can prevent those who are manifestly unfit from continuing their kind.")

Eugenics, Birth Control, and Abortion

Yet the history of eugenics is worth reflecting on, not least because the history of abortion cannot be divorced from it. Consider the case of Margaret Sanger, the founder of Planned Parenthood, who is still revered by it. While she herself opposed abortion, Planned Parenthood takes its support for it to be a straightforward extension of its support for birth control. And Sanger's crusade for birth control and "voluntary sterilization" was openly eugenicist.

She worried about the "increasing race of morons" in the United States, and complained that "a moron's vote" was just as good as that of his betters. She told the New York legislature that "the Jewish people and Italian families" were "filling the insane asylums" and "hospitals" and "feeble-minded institutions." Taxpayers were thus subsidizing the "multiplication of the unfit" when they should have been spending money "on geniuses." She condemned eighty-five million Americans as "mediocre to imbecile."

Lest we judge her too harshly, we should note that these sorts of sentiments were not unusual among the upper class and the intelligentsia in the first half of the last century. To take one example from hundreds: *The New Republic* editorialized in favor of contraception in a similar vein. "Few intelligent people would still maintain that it is better to have been born an imbecile than not to have been born at all." This "hideous doctrine," it continued, must be denounced "as a conspiracy by the superstitious against the race." The conspiracy resulted in "the multiplication of the unfit."

A Strange Idea of "Sacred"

This kind of thinking remained very much alive during the debate about abortion in the run-up to *Roe* [*v. Wade* (1973), the court case that legalized abortion]. The respected scientist Ashley Montagu wrote:

> If life is sacred . . . then it is about time we began treating it as such, instead of continuing to commit the frightful tragedies we do in permitting individuals to be brought into the world who will suffer all the days of their lives from seriously disabling defects . . . The initial basic right of the individual should be to be born without handicap. Anyone who, in the light of the facts, assists in bringing a seriously handicapped child into the world in my view commits a crime against humanity.

Abortion could prevent that "crime."

A similar view was expressed by [geneticist and columnist] Bentley Glass in his 1971 presidential address to the American Association for the Advancement of Science. Defending "the right of every child to be born with a sound physical and mental constitution, based on a sound genotype," he looked

Branded a Liability

In recent months [late 2007], people with Down syndrome and those who love and believe in them have shuddered at the advent of plans for expanded genetic prenatal testing. . . .

Although our policies over the past thirty years have become more supportive of people with Down syndrome, these children are increasingly seen as liabilities. . . . When parents knowingly choose to have such a child, the message they frequently receive from the larger society is that they have chosen wrongly. Imagine knowing that others believe your child should not exist.

Timothy Shriver,
"Silent Eugenics: Abortion and Down Syndrome,"
Commonweal, *November 9, 2007.*

forward to a "future time" when "[n]o parents will . . . have a right to burden society with a malformed or a mentally incompetent child."

The Eugenic Mindset

Traces, and more than traces, of the old eugenics live on in current attitudes and practices. The eugenic mindset has spread since *Roe*. It can be seen in the popularity of *Freakonomics* [a book of economic commentaries by Steven D. Levitt] and its speculations about abortion and crime. It can also be seen in the selective abortion of those whom we no longer label, but obviously still consider, the unfit.

We frown on abortion for the purpose of sex selection (although we don't prohibit it and it would be hard to do so while keeping abortion generally legal), in part because we think it expresses a negative view of women. We don't seem to have that worry about people with disabilities.

Health is a basic human good. It is perfectly understandable that disabilities should frighten (and sometimes even disgust) us. We might look at a disabled person and, comparing his condition to our own health, believe we wouldn't "want to live that way." This is especially true if we have more fears than knowledge about what life with a disability entails. Almost every parent of a disabled child would wish that his child not have a disability or that a cure be found. We are right to value health, but not by devaluing the unhealthy. Notice the way our language sometimes slips into identifying a person with his affliction, as in Elders's reference to "Down's syndrome infants." (We wouldn't call someone a "breast cancer woman.") The medical project should be to make people better, not to make better people.

Better Prospects for People with Down Syndrome

The improved condition of people with Down syndrome over the last few decades complicates both sides of the debate. Such people—at least those whom we allow to live—have better prospects than ever before. Their life expectancies have risen, and most of them can learn to read and hold a job (contrary to what some pregnant women are told). Our society treats disabled children and adults, in general, better than it used to, outside the contexts of abortion and euthanasia. So the worst pro-life fears about the dehumanization of the disabled have not been realized. It may be, of course, that our treatment of disabled children and adults would be even better if we did not routinely kill disabled fetuses in the womb.

But the same trends also make our treatment of disabled fetuses, in a way, more alarming. Down syndrome isn't a terminal illness, although it is a difficult (and expensive) condition. Yet we consider it something to be stamped out in the womb. We don't even protest at the starvation of infants who have it. In the "Baby Doe" case of 1982, a baby boy was born in Indiana with Down syndrome and a common symptom of that syndrome, an improperly formed esophagus. The boy's parents decided against surgery to fix the esophagus, opting instead to give him painkillers and let him die of starvation. The [Ronald] Reagan administration sought to intervene but was turned aside. It later promulgated regulations to ensure that babies receive medical care, but courts struck them down. Perhaps some future society, no doubt with its own smugness and its own sins, will condemn our barbarity.

Gifts or Commodities?

Or perhaps our eugenic tendencies will grow even stronger. One danger is that we will come to see children less as gifts than as products of manufacture. The commodification of human life is almost upon us: The biotech industry is looking at patenting early-stage human organisms pursuant to stem-cell research. Will we grow less and less tolerant of what we see as defective goods? Will we abort children who are deaf, or blind, or dumb, or short, or gay? How will the health and insurance industries treat us if we don't? How will our neighbors—or the strangers that we meet?

All over this country, there are people sitting in seminars at think tanks, colleges, and working groups, pondering these questions as though they concern the future. But these evils already exist, in embryonic form, today. Just ask Patricia Bauer. Or listen to Joycelyn Elders.

Doctors and Abortion

The party of death [the Democrats] has corrupted the practice of medicine, turning healers into killers. Bernard Nathanson made that journey, and returned.

Nathanson was one of the founders of the National Association for Repeal of Abortion Laws. In the 1970s, he directed what was at the time the largest abortion clinic in the world, the Center for Reproductive and Sexual Health in Manhattan. He performed, he says, "many thousands" of abortions.

It was not a religious conversion, but technological and scientific advances, that changed his mind. His thinking about abortion, like that of many other people, was powerfully affected by the development of ultrasound technology. "When ultrasound in the early 1970s confronted me with the sight of the embryo in the womb, I simply lost my faith in abortion on demand," he later wrote. He was, at the time, an atheist.

It was not only the images that swayed him, but the new understanding of fetal development that ultrasound made possible. "As recently as [1969], we knew almost nothing of the fetus; when abortion on demand was unleashed in the United States, fetology essentially did not exist."

A Close Look at the Violence

Nathanson went on to become a pro-life author, speaker, and documentary producer. His 1985 film *The Silent Scream* is misremembered today. It was not primarily an attempt to prove that abortion inflicts pain on a fetus (exactly when the fetus develops to the point of feeling pain is still a disputed question). It was a depiction of the violence of abortion.

> By 1984 . . . I had begun to ask myself more questions about abortion: What actually goes on in an abortion? I had done many, but abortion is a blind procedure. The doctor does not see what he is doing. He puts an instrument into a uterus and he turns on a motor, and a suction machine goes on and something is vacuumed out; it ends up as a little pile of meat in a gauze bag. I wanted to know what happened, so in 1984 I said to a friend of mine, who was doing fifteen or maybe twenty abortions a day, "Look, do me a favor, Jay. Next Saturday, when you are doing all these abortions, put an ultrasound device on the mother and tape it for me."

He did, and when he looked at the tapes with me in an editing studio, he was so affected that he never did another abortion.

> *"Genetic screening was developed by medical geneticists to help the genetically 'unfit,' precisely the people the eugenicists would have sterilized, have as many children as they wanted."*

Prenatal Testing for Genetic Disorders Should Not Be Equated with Eugenics

Ruth Schwartz Cowan

In the following viewpoint, Ruth Schwartz Cowan argues that medical genetics is not "eugenic" because eugenics seek to prevent potential carriers of "bad" genes from reproducing, whereas medical genetics help people, including carriers, reproduce free from fear. Moreover, prenatal screening may actually reduce abortions among carriers of single gene mutations who may abort primarily out of fear that the fetus might *have a disorder. Cowan is a professor of history and sociology of science at the University of Pennsylvania in Philadelphia; her specialties include genetics. She is the author of* Heredity and Hope.

Ruth Schwartz Cowan, "Medical Genetics Is Not Eugenics," *Heredity and Hope: The Case for Genetic Screening*, pp. 234–240, 245. Copyright © 2008 by the President and Fellows of Harvard College. Reprinted by permission of the publisher.

As you read, consider the following questions:

1. According to Cowan, what were the "formative years" of medical genetics?
2. How does Cowan define "the chief goal of the eugenicists"?
3. According to Cowan, medical genetics provides what "hope that many parents never had before"?

The connection that critics make between medical genetics and eugenics is historically fallacious. Activists on the political right are as mistaken as activists on the political left: Genetic screening was not eugenics in the past, is not eugenics in the present, and, unless its technological systems become radically transformed, will not be eugenics in the future. The technologies of medical genetics were not constructed with eugenic goals, and the practices of medical genetics will not produce eugenic results—neither directly through the actions of medical experts nor indirectly, as the sociologist Troy Duster likes to say, through the "backdoor" of patients' compliance with experts' instructions.

There is, to start with, no meaningful historical connection between the enterprise once called eugenics and the enterprise now called medical genetics. There were certainly some Mendelian [early] geneticists who were eugenicists, but the vast majority of classical geneticists figured out, early on, that most of the eugenic claims made about the inheritance of feeblemindedness and alcoholism were, if not entirely false, then at least undemonstrated. Human genetics, the genetics of probability and statistics in large populations, the genetics of allelic [gene form variety] frequencies and mutation incidences, indeed had some eugenicists among its founding fathers and mothers, but medical genetics owes very little to it.

A Medical Specialty

Medical genetics is, first and foremost, a medical specialty. During the formative years of the specialty, roughly between

1960 and 1980, most physicians were not interested enough in human genetics to take the trouble to understand it, largely because human genetics was then focused on evolutionary questions, not on matters pertinent to clinical practice.

The foundational science for medical genetics is classical Mendelian genetics: the genetics of dominant and recessive genes strung like beads along chromosomes. This is the genetics that provided the foundation on which the technological systems of genetic screening—newborn screening, carrier screening, prenatal diagnosis—were built. Classical geneticists were not, by and large, eugenicists, and neither were the physician who constructed those systems on the foundation that the geneticists laid. By the time molecular genetics, the genetics of DNA and RNA, of sequences of molecules and production of proteins, had advanced far enough to be useful for screening purposes (the mutation that produces sickling hemoglobin was the first mutation whose location was pinpointed, in 1978), the technologies of genetic screening had been routinized for more than a decade. Some of the scientists who lobbied for funding of the Human Genome Initiative may have used the rhetoric of eugenics when speaking to venture capitalists, legislators, and bureaucrats, but most of them (for example, Robert Sinsheimer, Joshua Lederberg, and James Watson) were molecular biologists, not medical geneticists; they had no medical training or clinical experience, and they played no role whatsoever in the development of the technological systems through which genetic screening is practiced.

Differences in Major Goals

Technological systems are built to achieve certain goals; those goals get hard-wired, as it were, into the components of the system. The chief goal of the eugenicists, "improvement of the race," was never one of the goals of genetic screening—and it did not become one, even after genomic research had identified the locations of dozens of disease-causing mutations. The

Resistance to Genetic Testing

Thanks to advances in genetic testing and prenatal screening, science is winning the war against ailments that have plagued mankind for centuries. But mankind may not want the victories.

As scientific breakthroughs tumble out of America's research labs, resistance to medical advances is gathering momentum, said Steven Miles, a medical ethics expert at the University of Minnesota [based in Minneapolis] and past president of the American Society for Bioethics and Humanities. . . .

"To compare [Down syndrome] to eye color trivializes the nature of this condition," he said.

"Half these kids have some kind of heart defect. Ten percent have their intestines blocked. They have serious eye problems, hearing problems, thyroid problems."

Jennifer Miller, "How Perfect Should Our Children Be?"
September 24, 2007. www.bioethicsinternational.org.

founders of eugenics differed about which race they had in mind: Some meant "the white race," some "the German race," some "the Mexican race," and some, even, "the human race." The founders of medical genetics, however, made deliberate efforts to separate themselves from what [twentieth-century geneticist] James Neel called "the parlous [perilous] intellectual state" of eugenic research and practice because they thought it politically and scientifically correct to do so.

From the very beginning, the founders of medical genetics—people like Neel, Fritz Fuchs, Michael Kaback, and Robert Guthrie—viewed their basic project as the relief of human suffering, not improvement of the race. Relief of suffering might, in their view, also improve the health of races or populations or societies, but improving the health and well-being of individuals was always their primary goal. Some of the individuals they wanted to help were people who had already borne children who were struggling with painful and disabling diseases like β-thalassemia or muscular dystrophy. Geneticists wanted to reduce the suffering of both parents and children by helping the parents to have additional children, and by ensuring that those additional children would be free of the disease. Other individuals who could be helped were those who knew themselves to be at risk and were repressing their desire to have children for fear that the risk would become reality, that the risk status of the parent would be visited upon the child.

Helping the "Genetically Unfit" to Reproduce Safely

The reproductive goals of medical genetics are thus precisely the opposite of those of eugenics. Eugenicists wanted to ensure that the people they defined as genetically unfit did not reproduce; that is why they pushed for sterilization and segregation. Genetic screening was developed by medical geneticists to help the genetically "unfit," precisely the people the eugenicists would have sterilized, have as many children as they wanted. The earliest patients who were referred to medical geneticists for counseling were people who suspected (or whose doctors suspected) that they carried the genes for serious diseases. Prenatal diagnosis was developed to assure those worried patients that they could have children free of the disease they feared. To put the matter another way: The practices of genetic screening are inherently pronatalist. By supporting parental hopes for reasonably healthy children, they encourage at-risk couples to reproduce.

The presumed connection between eugenics and medical genetics is not the only criticism of genetic screening that turns out to be historically ill founded; there are several others. Reproductive feminists claim, for example, that genetic-screening techniques were developed by inappropriate experimentation on women's bodies—but it seems unlikely that [Danish physician] Fritz Fuchs's first amniocentesis patient, who was able to carry her pregnancy to term without fearing that she would give birth to a boy with hemophilia, or the several dozen Cypriot women who subjected themselves to fetoscopy to ensure that they would not raise another child with thalassemia [a genetic disorder that interferes with blood production], would agree.

Not Discrimination Against the Disabled

Disability activists claim that genetic screening is a form of discrimination against the disabled—but it seems unlikely that the parents who banded together to form associations like the National Tay-Sachs Disease Association or the Cyprus Anti-Anaemic Society or the National Association of Retarded Citizens would agree.

Disability activists also worry that as genetic screening diminishes the number of children born with disabilities, services to disabled people will decrease. There is no evidence to suggest that this has happened, even though screening programs have existed for decades. In Cyprus, discrimination against thalassemic people has lessened as the number of babies born with the disease has fallen. In the United States, school systems have been required to provide special educational services for disabled children, and all kinds of public facilities have been modified to accommodate their needs—in the same years that prenatal diagnosis became common practice. In most states, legislation has made it illegal for insurance companies to drop clients who decide to go forward with pregnancies after receiving worrying prenatal diagnoses. Contrary to what some disability activists assume, many people support widening the rights of disabled children and adults while simultaneously believing that abortion for fetal indications is morally wise.

Motherhood Concepts and Genetic Screening

Reproductive feminists have also claimed that what they call selective abortion violates the essential morality of motherhood, turning the ideal of nurturing care into the ideal of quality control. The legions of feminists (as well as the legions of women who are not feminists) who have sought—and even sued to get—prenatal diagnosis for Down syndrome are not likely to agree with them. Such women are, indeed, rejecting some traditional ideas about motherhood, particularly the notion that the ideal mother is willing to sacrifice herself for her children. By choosing prenatal diagnosis and the possibility of abortion, such women are asserting that they would prefer not to sacrifice themselves to caring for a chronically dependent, suffering child, and that there are other significant social roles that they hope to play in the course of their lives—spouse, employee, friend, athlete—that would be very difficult or impossible to combine with such care. Many of these women have put off childbearing to complete their educations or build employment résumés, which means that they are at increased risk of bearing a child with Down syndrome.

Reproductive feminists and abortion opponents have also argued against genetic screening on the grounds that it increases the frequency of abortion—but it is unlikely that women (and men, for that matter) who know they are carriers of single-gene mutations will see it quite the same way. Were it not for prenatal diagnosis, these people might terminate all the pregnancies they carried or caused to be carried. The physicians who created thalassemia-screening programs on Cyprus would not agree either; they knew how often the parents of their patients were terminating pregnancies.

New Hope

Genetic screening increases reproductive choice, and it also provides hope, hope that many parents never had before—hope of having, not a perfect child, but a child who, at least at the start of life, is free of devastating disease or overwhelming disability. Screening has become a routine practice in many different countries, and in many different social circumstances, for precisely these good reasons. Negative consequences, for individuals or for the ethnic communities to which they belong or for the national societies of which they are citizens, have been rare. Surely, then, the time has come for prospective parents to stop feeling guilty about participating in screening, and for historians, social scientists, and journalists to stop warning about its hidden eugenic evils. Those evils do not exist—and continuing to insist that they do is an attempt to further a political agenda by making good people feel unnecessarily guilty about their fundamentally wise and moral behavior.

Periodical Bibliography

The following articles have been selected to supplement the diverse views presented in this chapter.

Stylianos E. Antonarakis and Jacques S. Beckmann
"Mendelian Disorders Deserve More Attention," *Nature Reviews Genetics*, April 2006.

Elizabeth Bassett
"Genetic Testing Gains Ground as Safeguards Increase," *Fort Worth Business Press*, May 12, 2008.

Christianity Today
"The Slope Really Is Slippery," March 2007.

Economist
"Wanted: Perfection," July 7, 2007.

Timothy Krahn
"Where Are We Going with Preimplantation Genetic Diagnosis?" *CMAJ: Canadian Medical Association Journal Supplement*, May 8, 2007.

Jessica Long
"Genetic Testing Exposes Insurance Industry to Ethical Dilemmas," *San Diego Business Journal*, October 23, 2006.

Elizabeth R. Schiltz
"Confessions of a 'Genetic Outlaw,'" *Human Life Review*, Summer/Fall 2006.

Jackie Leach Scully, Rouven Porz, and Christoph Rehmann-Sutter
"'You Don't Make Genetic Test Decisions from One Day to the Next'—Using Time to Preserve Moral Space," *Bioethics*, May 2007.

Valerie Uline
"The Temptation to Test: Parents Could Screen Children for Genetic Diseases, but Letting a Child Decide Later Might Be Better. Early Detection Doesn't Mean a Cure, and Knowing Could Be a Burden," *Los Angeles Times*, March 3, 2008.

University of Michigan
"Newborn Screening: New Technology Revives Old Controversy," August 20, 2007. www.emaxhealth.com.

CHAPTER 4

What Is the Medical Future of Genetic Disorders?

Chapter Preface

As genetic research advances, hope for eradicating many disorders is growing ever stronger. But the road to genetic perfection is full of ethical and scientific controversy. Often the public seems mixed in its response to stem cell research.

In the elections of November 2007, New Jersey—which in 2004 had become the first state to fund stem cell research through taxes—placed on its ballot a proposal to allocate an additional $450 million for such research. Advance polls "indicated that New Jersey voters were likely to pass [the 2007 proposal] by a margin of 57 percent to 36 percent," yet the actual vote "defeated the stem-cell referendum by a vote of 53 percent to 47 percent," lamented Parkinsons Alliance chair Marty Tuchman in the wake of that election. "All of the voters who stayed home ... may someday be reminded of it when the doctor walks through the door and tells them that they or someone they love does indeed have a fearsome disease."

Why did New Jersey voters reject something the New Jersey public apparently favored? "People on both sides of the stem cell debate said the key factor in New Jersey's failed initiative was taxpayer fatigue," wrote Terri Somers of the *San Diego Union-Tribune*. "Taxpayers were not keen on taking on more debt. . . . [Moreover,] voter turnout was low, with no major statewide races at stake. In such years, opponents of a measure are much more likely to go to the polls than those who support a measure."

Stem cell research is controversial largely because much—though not all—of it uses tissue from human embryos in ways that are fatal to the embryos; hence, those who believe human life begins at conception oppose embryonic research for the same reasons they oppose abortion. "Harvesting these 'embryonic stem cells' involves the deliberate killing of innocent human beings, a gravely immoral act," read a 2008 statement issued by the United States Conference of Catholic Bishops. "Yet some try to justify it by appealing to a hoped-for future benefit to others."

Even aside from direct-harm issues, the whole idea of genetic manipulation can be frightening. This concluding chapter explores its ramifications, along with other genetic issues that may help determine humanity's future.

"*I have no doubt that most people . . . are certain that human genetic improvement is a bad idea, but I'd like to shake up that certainty.*"

Prenatal Gene Manipulation Has Many Advantages

Ronald M. Green

In the following viewpoint, Ronald M. Green answers four major objections to the concept of "building babies" through gene engineering, arguing that basic human nature counters the possibility that parental love or people's appreciation of their natural abilities will decline; that a society making extensive use of gene manipulation is as likely to move toward egalitarianism as toward oligarchy; and that no religion expressly forbids genetic engineering. Green is adjunct professor of community and family medicine and faculty director of the Ethics Institute at Dartmouth College in New Hampshire. His books include Babies by Design: The Ethics of Genetic Choice.

As you read, consider the following questions:

1. What British agency approves requests for preimplantation genetic diagnosis?

Ronald M. Green, "Design," *The Washington Post*, April 13, 2008, p. B1. Copyright © 2008 The Washington Post Company. Reproduced by permission of the author.

2. What 1997 science fiction film focused on concerns about societal eugenic obsessions?

3. According to Green, what would be the real cause of the problem in a situation where a child was unfairly pressured to live up to his or her genetic potential?

The two British couples no doubt thought that their appeal for medical help in conceiving a child was entirely reasonable. Over several generations, many female members of their families had died of breast cancer. One or both spouses in each couple had probably inherited the genetic mutations for the disease, and they wanted to use in-vitro fertilization and preimplantation genetic diagnosis (PGD) to select only the healthy embryos for implantation. Their goal was to eradicate breast cancer from their family lines once and for all.

In the United States, this combination of reproductive and genetic medicine—what one scientist has dubbed "reprogenetics"—remains largely unregulated, but Britain has a formal agency, the Human Fertilization and Embryology Authority (HFEA), that must approve all requests for PGD. In July 2007, after considerable deliberation, the HFEA approved the procedure for both families. The concern was not about the use of PGD to avoid genetic disease, since embryo screening for serious disorders is commonplace now on both sides of the Atlantic. What troubled the HFEA was the fact that an embryo carrying the cancer mutation could go on to live for 40 or 50 years before ever developing cancer, and there was a chance it might never develop. Did this warrant selecting and discarding embryos? To its critics, the HFEA, in approving this request, crossed a bright line separating legitimate medical genetics from the quest for "the perfect baby."

Search for the "$1,000 Genome"

Like it or not, that decision is a sign of things to come—and not necessarily a bad sign. Since the completion of the Human Genome Project in 2003, our understanding of the genetic bases of human disease and non-disease traits has been growing almost exponentially. The National Institutes of Health has initiated a quest for the "$1,000 genome," a 10-year program to develop machines that could identify all the genetic letters in anyone's genome at low cost (it took more than $3 billion to sequence the first human genome). With this technology, which some believe may be just four or five years away, we could not only scan an individual's—or embryo's—genome, we could also rapidly compare thousands of people and pinpoint those DNA sequences or combinations that underlie the variations that contribute to our biological differences.

With knowledge comes power. If we understand the genetic causes of obesity, for example, we can intervene by means of embryo selection to produce a child with a reduced genetic likelihood of getting fat. Eventually, without discarding embryos at all, we could use gene-targeting techniques to tweak fetal DNA sequences. No child would have to face a lifetime of dieting or experience the health and cosmetic problems associated with obesity. The same is true for cognitive problems such as dyslexia. Geneticists have already identified some of the mutations that contribute to this disorder. Why should a child struggle with reading difficulties when we could alter the genes responsible for the problem?

A Real-Life Gattaca?

Many people are horrified at the thought of such uses of genetics, seeing echoes of the 1997 science-fiction film *Gattaca*, which depicted a world where parents choose their children's traits. Human weakness has been eliminated through genetic engineering, and the few parents who opt for a "natural" conception run the risk of producing offspring—"invalids" or "degenerates"—who become members of a despised underclass. Gattaca's world is clean and efficient, but its eugenic obsessions have all but extinguished human love and compassion.

These fears aren't limited to fiction. Over the past few years, many bioethicists have spoken out against genetic manipulations. The critics tend to voice at least four major concerns. First, they worry about the effect of genetic selection on parenting. Will our ability to choose our children's biological inheritance lead parents to replace unconditional love with a consumerist mentality that seeks perfection?

Second, they ask whether gene manipulations will diminish our freedom by making us creatures of our genes or our parents' whims. In his book *Enough*, the techno-critic Bill McKibben asks: If I am a world-class runner, but my parents inserted the "Sweatworks2010 GenePack" in my genome, can I really feel pride in my accomplishments? Worse, if I refuse to use my costly genetic endowments, will I face relentless pressure to live up to my parents' expectations?

Beware the Horrors of Eugenics

Third, many critics fear that reproductive genetics will widen our social divisions as the affluent "buy" more competitive abilities for their offspring. Will we eventually see "speciation," the emergence of two or more human populations so different that they no longer even breed with one another? Will we recreate the horrors of eugenics that led, in Europe, Asia and the United States, to the sterilization of tens of thousands of people declared to be "unfit" and that in Nazi Germany paved the way for the Holocaust?

Finally, some worry about the religious implications of this technology. Does it amount to a forbidden and prideful "playing God"?

To many, the answers to these questions are clear. Not long ago, when I asked a large class at Dartmouth Medical School [Hanover, New Hampshire] whether they thought that

Web-Surf Your Own DNA

A Silicon Valley startup, 23andMe, is named after the number of paired chromosomes in every human. In stealth mode until a launch planned for later this year [2007], 23andMe is using powerful gene-reading chips to build a company that is among several hoping to cash in on personalized genomics—the tailoring of an individual's health care and lifestyle based on DNA and biomarkers.

When 23andMe goes live, customers will be asked to spit into short plastic tubes or to swab cells from inside their cheeks and mail in the sample. 23andMe will then analyze the data in relation to reams of information about ailments, treatments, diet, and ancestry and compare the results with those of thousands of others who have been tested for genes associated with diseases and other traits.

The cybersynthesis will be channeled into a customized DNA diary on the Web site. The company is considering a feature that would allow people to then link their personalized pages to those of others who share their DNA—fellow sprinters, say, or people at risk for Alzheimer's—just as you can now link to college chums on Facebook. 23andMe has not discussed pricing, but competitors are talking about charging upwards of $2,000 a person. . . .

David Ewing Duncan, "Welcome to the Future,"
Condé Nast Portfolio, *November 2007.*

we should move in the direction of human genetic engineering, more than 80 percent said no. This squares with public opinion polls that show a similar degree of opposition. Nevertheless, "babies by design" are probably in our future—but I think that the critics' concerns may be less troublesome than they first appear.

The Dangers Are Likely Exaggerated

Will critical scrutiny replace parental love? Not likely. Even today, parents who hope for a healthy child but have one born with disabilities tend to love that child ferociously. The very intensity of parental love is the best protection against its erosion by genetic technologies. Will a child somehow feel less free because parents have helped select his or her traits? The fact is that a child is already remarkably influenced by the genes she inherits. The difference is that we haven't taken control of the process. Yet.

Knowing more about our genes may actually increase our freedom by helping us understand the biological obstacles—and opportunities—we have to work with. Take the case of Tiger Woods. His father, Earl, is said to have handed him a golf club when he was still in the playpen. Earl probably also gave Tiger the genes for some of the traits that help make him a champion golfer. Genes and upbringing worked together to inspire excellence. Does Tiger feel less free because of his inherited abilities? Did he feel pressured by his parents? I doubt it. Of course, his story could have gone the other way, with overbearing parents forcing a child into their mold. But the problem in that case wouldn't be genetics, but bad parenting.

Fear of a "Genobility"

Granted, the social effects of reproductive genetics are worrisome. The risks of producing a "genobility," genetic overlords ruling a vast genetic underclass, are real. But genetics could also become a tool for reducing the class divide. Will we see the day when perhaps all youngsters are genetically vaccinated against dyslexia? And how might this contribute to everyone's social betterment?

As for the question of intruding on God's domain, the answer is less clear than the critics believe. The use of genetic medicine to cure or prevent disease is widely accepted by religious traditions, even those that oppose discarding embryos. Speaking in 1982 at the Pontifical Academy of Sciences [headquartered in the Vatican], Pope John Paul II observed that modern biological research "can ameliorate the condition of those who are affected by chromosomic diseases," and he lauded this as helping to cure "the smallest and weakest of human beings . . . during their intrauterine life or in the period immediately after birth." For Catholicism and some other traditions, it is one thing to cure disease, but another to create children who are faster runners, longer-lived or smarter.

Improving on Human Nature

But why should we think that the human genome is a once-and-for-all-finished, untamperable product? All of the biblically derived faiths permit human beings to improve on nature using technology, from agriculture to aviation. Why not improve our genome? I have no doubt that most people considering these questions for the first time are certain that human genetic improvement is a bad idea, but I'd like to shake up that certainty.

Genomic science is racing toward a future in which foreseeable improvements include reduced susceptibility to a host of diseases, increased life span, better cognitive functioning and maybe even cosmetic enhancements such as whiter, straighter teeth. Yes, genetic orthodontics may be in our future. The challenge is to see that we don't also unleash the demons of discrimination and oppression. Although I acknowledge the risks, I believe that we can and will incorporate gene technology into the ongoing human adventure.

| "*'Geneticism' is particularly tempting to conservatives, because it appears to provide scientific support for the idea of an innate human nature. . . . But this temptation should be resisted.*"

Genetic Advancements May Not Meet Expectations

Jim Manzi

Looking at the contemporary tendency to claim a genetic basis for every emotion and behavior, Jim Manzi, in the following viewpoint, warns of inherent dangers such as a potential drift toward the same social Darwinism that attempted to establish a scientific basis for racism. He also explains how complicated a truly comprehensive understanding of genes would be. Manzi is former CEO of Massachusetts-based Lotus Software (formerly Lotus Development Corporation and now a branch of IBM), and has been actively involved with several other technological businesses. His other articles for National Review *and* National Review Online *include "The Right Formula: Conservatives and Science."*

Jim Manzi, "Undetermined," *National Review*, vol. 60, June 2, 2008, pp. 26–32. Copyright © 2008 by National Review, Inc., 215 Lexington Avenue, New York, NY 10016. Reproduced by permission.

As you read, consider the following questions:

1. What broadcasting network ran the story, "Eureka: Happiness Gene Found"?

2. According to Manzi, how many of the average person's twenty thousand genes are linked to the regulation of brain function?

3. What does Manzi note as one major flaw in the Minnesota Transracial Adoption Study?

Driven by the genetic revolution, biology has displaced physics as the world's most important and exciting science. A substantial majority of all U.S. academic-research spending in science and engineering is now in life sciences. More than twice as many of the developed world's most widely cited scientific research papers are in the life sciences as are in physics and chemistry combined. Successful new scientific paradigms change how we see the world, and therefore exert intellectual influence well outside of the technical specialties that produced them. The more fundamental the paradigm, the wider and deeper are these radiating influences. In the case of modern biology, they are profound. Proceeding from the sociobiology movement of the 1970s, some biologists have sought to explain all individual behavior and social organization as the predictable result of genes-plus-environment. The reigning presumption of academic America is that over time this movement will sweep all before it.

This perspective inevitably trickles down into mainstream opinion. To choose just a few illustrative examples, within the past few months [early 2008] both *Time* and *The New York Times Magazine* have had cover stories on the evolutionary roots of morality; *Time* has had a second cover story on the biological basis of romance; *Newsweek* has had one article on the genetic explanation of psychological resilience and another arguing that varying incidences of disease-causing pathogens explain the degree to which different countries' policies are individualist or collectivist; NBC News has broadcast a story on the genetic basis for smoking addiction; ABC has had a story on the evolutionary origins of the incest taboo; and CBS has run a story titled "Eureka: Happiness Gene Found." Mass media are inundated with this biology-explains-all ideology.

Old Thoughts, New Errors

Now, the idea that the vast majority of people share a set of stable, inherent characteristics—that is, the idea that there is such a thing as human nature—is not new. Nor are the subsidiary ideas that individuals have somewhat varying inborn natures; that this variation is partially heritable; and that individuals who share a lineage will demonstrate common traits and tendencies. All of these beliefs are at least several thousand years old, and probably predate written records.

What's new is that—because we believe that we have uncovered at least a component of the physical manifestation of human nature, in the form of the genome—many now believe that we can *operationalize* these old ideas: that we can explain the causes of the behaviors of individuals and groups sufficiently to predict these behaviors scientifically. Those who believe this, believe that we can remove the mind-body problem from the purview of philosophy by reducing the mind to a scientifically explained physical phenomenon. When pushed, such theorists will generally admit that we cannot yet do much of this, but will then state confidently that we "are starting to understand" or "are on the verge of explaining" various human behaviors.

A Gene for Everything

Media outlets will often speak loosely of things such as a "happiness gene," a "gay gene," or a "smart gene." The state-of-the-art method for finding such a link is something called a "genome-wide association study" (GWAS). In a GWAS, scientists use blood or saliva samples to sequence the DNA for a group of several thousand people who exhibit a trait or behavior of interest (the "case group"), and for a second group of several thousand who do not exhibit the trait or behavior (the "control group"). Scientists then look for genetic differences between the two groups. In cases where a single malfunctioning gene creates, for example, a catastrophic disease that overwhelms other genetic and environmental factors, a GWAS can quickly pinpoint the culprit. Sometimes, however, the behavior or trait is caused by several interacting genes—so that, for example, Gene 1 has some effect only if Gene 2 has a special structure. This is called "epistatic interaction," and can involve a large number of genes. Epistatic interactions make genetic effects harder to identify. Scientists deal with this problem and others by creating larger and larger case and control groups. The scaling up of such studies is among the most exciting frontiers in genetics. It is essentially an engineering problem, and money poured into solving it will likely improve human health through genetic screening and, ultimately, therapies.

The Structural Limits of GWAS

Seeing this momentum, it is natural to assume that eventually we will have explained *all* human behavior, not just diseases caused by one or a small number of interacting genes. But the GWAS technique hits structural limits when applied to conditions that involve epistatic interactions among lots of genes. Mental activity is now widely believed by scientists to depend on many genes (though mental illnesses such as schizophrenia or bipolar disorder may turn out to be partial exceptions). A person has about 20,000 genes, of which more than 5,000 are believed to play some role in regulating brain function. Consider a simplified case in which some personality characteristic—aggressiveness, for example—is regulated by 100 genes, each of which can have two possible states ("on" or "off"). The combinatorial math is daunting: There are more than a trillion trillion possible combinations of these gene states. Thus we could sequence the DNA of all 6.7 billion human beings and still not know which genes are responsible for aggressiveness.

Association, Not Cause

A second limitation of a GWAS is that it detects association rather than causation. Suppose we found that a case group of persons suffering from a disease had a greater incidence of some gene than did a control group, but that we failed to notice that the case group was disproportionately of Chinese ancestry. Culturally transmitted behaviors in the case group might be responsible for the disease, even if these behaviors had nothing to do with the gene in question. That is, the gene could be nothing more than a marker for Chinese ancestry, and hence for participation in behaviors that cause the disease. Geneticists call this problem "stratification," and deal with it by carefully matching individuals in the case and control groups to ensure that the groups really are comparable. The problem is that these stratification effects can be fiendishly subtle. No matter how carefully we match cases with controls, there can always be some unobserved environmental factor correlated with, but not caused by, a genetic difference between groups, and this environmental factor might be what is actually causing the disease.

The Complexity of Reality

Further, to think in terms of genes is to abstract away from a biochemical reality that is far more complex. On one hand, a gene is not an atomic entity, but a sophisticated machine with many components. Much as in the progress of particle physics over the past century, we keep discovering components-within-components of the genetic mechanism that are relevant to physical and mental outcomes, and it's entirely plausible that we will eventually get all the way down to subatomic quan-

Altruistic Research Becomes Big Business

Guangping Gao, then a graduate student at Florida International University working under the tutelage of [researcher Rajinder] Kaul, succeeded in cloning the Canavan gene by early 1993. The research drew on tissue samples provided to [research director Reuben] Matalon by over a hundred families from around the world who had been stricken by the disease. . . .

Unbeknownst to the families involved, a patent application was filed in September 1994, and U.S. Patent No. 5,679,635 was issued to the MCH [Miami Children Hospital] Research Institute [where much of the research had been conducted] in October 1997. The MCH began to develop a marketing plan for its patent. . . .

. . . These families—who had actively participated in Matalon's research enterprise in hopes of helping families like them avoid the ravages of Canavan disease—were thus dumbfounded when the MCH was issued a U.S. patent covering the genetic test for the disease and began to enforce it. Not only were the families uninformed about the scope of their research participation, they were betrayed by the ultimate commercialization and profiteering of the institution they believed was motivated, as were they, by altruism and the desire to help prevent this terrible disease.

Karen F. Greif and Jon F. Merz, "Who Owns the Genome? The Patenting of Human Genes," Current Controversies in the Biological Sciences: Case Studies of Policy & Challenges from New Technologies. *Cambridge, MA: MIT Press, 2007.*

tum effects as drivers of behavior. On the other hand, as we move away from the genome itself, we see that other dimly understood biochemical processes have a large impact on how the information contained in the gene gets expressed as an observable human characteristic. And all of this is before we consider interactions of the human organism as a whole with those factors that we typically term "environmental," ranging from nutrition and exposure to pathogens to parenting styles and childhood experiences. . . .

Consider a prominent example of the debate over genetic causality: the assertion that there is a genetic basis for IQ differences between racial groups. Because it is both so consequential and so fraught with emotion, this claim has been subject to an almost unique degree of critical scrutiny, descending into the kind of irresolvable debate that we see in economics and the social sciences.

No Physical Pathway

Let's start with some facts. There are sustained, statistically significant differences in IQ-test performance between self-identified racial groups in the U.S., and these self-identified racial groups also have statistically significant differences in genetic content. But those who assert that these genetic differences *cause* the difference in test scores have never been able to demonstrate a physical pathway from genes to IQ. In the absence of such a demonstration, they have had instead to rely on those old standbys, twin and adoption studies. (The logic here is that these studies can control for either genetics or the environment. Identical twins have identical DNA. By looking at cases of adoption, meanwhile, researchers can study children whose genetic background differs from that of the families in which they are raised.) The most famous and rigorous such study was the Minnesota Transracial Adoption Study [1976] of families in which high-IQ white parents adopted black, white, or mixed-race children. In theory, studying these subjects should have allowed us to isolate the influence of genes on intelligence by measuring the IQs of children in each group after they had been raised in approximately equal environments. But it turned out that the environments were not even close to equal. The black children had been adopted at later ages than the white children, and this can plausibly be associated with differing scores on IQ tests.

Heredity or Environment?

The Minnesota study provides a good illustration of why it is so difficult to separate genetic from environmental effects: No such experiment in a non-totalitarian society is sufficiently controlled to support reasonable inferences. When we use these methods to try to understand the causes of IQ differences between groups, we are like cavemen trying to figure out how a computer works by poking at it with sharpened sticks. This, not political correctness, is why the American Psychological Association's consensus on the matter of race and IQ is that, "at present, this question has no scientific answer."

When we carefully consider assertions of a genetic basis for other mental or social phenomena, this pattern emerges time and again. The explanation sounds plausible—it *might* be true—but we can't be sure. Is the almost-universal human religious impulse a byproduct of evolution? Perhaps. Can altruism be explained fully by genetic competition? Could be. Does homosexuality have a genetic cause? It's possible.

Sound the Warning

The fallacy of what might be called "geneticism" is particularly tempting to conservatives, because it appears to provide scientific support for the idea of an innate human nature—an idea that has long been assaulted from the left. But this temptation should be resisted. If the pretense to scientific knowledge is always dangerous, it is doubly so when wedded to state power, because it leads to pseudo-rational interventions that unduly extend authority and restrict freedom. That the linkage of race and IQ is provocative to contemporary audiences is not surprising: It is almost a direct restatement, in the language of genetics, of the key premise of Social Darwinism. That prior attempt to apply beliefs about human nature to public policy [notably in the forced sterilization of "undesirables" in the early twentieth century] should be a cautionary tale for our era.

> *"As genetic testing becomes faster, easier, and more common, more prospective parents will . . . be looking for ways to cure [genetic] diseases . . . [through] in utero gene therapy."*

Gene Therapy Could Eradicate Genetic Disorders

Ramez Naam

In this selection, Ramez Naam looks at recent advances in genetic engineering and gene therapy. With prenatal genetic testing now widely accepted and becoming increasingly simple and accurate, he predicts that in utero gene therapy, and the changing of dangerous genes into healthy ones, will become possible and accepted in the foreseeable future. Naam, who helped develop Windows' Explorer and Outlook programs, is currently group program manager of Microsoft's Live Search. He also works as an adviser to various technical associations and is a regular speaker at technology and futures conferences.

As you read, consider the following questions:

1. What was "the first genetically engineered primate"?

Ramez Naam, *More Than Human: Embracing the Promise of Biological Enhancement.* New York: Broadway Books, 2005. Copyright © 2005 by Ramez Naam. All rights reserved. Used by permission of Broadway Books, a division of Random House, Inc.

2. What agency turned down a 1998 proposal to perform in utero gene therapy?

3. According to Naam, at what fetal age will Tay-Sachs disease soon be detectable?

• • • To date, no one has altered the genes of a human embryo. The closest researchers have come to this is a rhesus monkey named ANDi. ANDi was the first genetically engineered primate brought into this world. Her creators took a rhesus monkey egg and inserted a jellyfish gene, one that makes jellyfish glow green. The gene is in every cell in ANDi's body. By inserting a foreign gene into an embryo of such a close relative of ours, scientists have demonstrated that genetically engineering human embryos is nearly feasible.

The technique for genetically engineering an embryo is similar to gene therapy: scientists use a gene vector to deliver a new gene to the embryo in essentially the same way they would deliver a new gene to any other cell. Scientifically and technologically, the two techniques are almost the same.

There are important differences in the results produced when a gene is inserted at such an early stage, though. To illustrate these differences, let's compare ANDi, the genetically engineered monkey we just talked about, and Ashanti DeSilva, the first human to receive gene therapy.

ANDi went through *germline genetic engineering.* She had a new gene inserted into her when she was just a single fertilized cell. That gene integrated itself into the DNA of that single cell, and from then on, every time that cell and its daughter cells divided and made new copies, the new DNA was copied too. Consequently, every cell in ANDi's body carries the jellyfish protein gene, and if ANDi has children, she has a 50 percent chance of passing that gene on to them as well. Her germline—the genetic information she can convey to future generations—has been engineered, hence the term germline genetic engineering.

Ashanti, on the other hand, underwent *somatic gene therapy*. She was four years old when it happened. By this time, Ashanti's body was made up of trillions of cells. Delivering the new gene to every one of her cells was effectively impossible, so researchers focused on just the most critical cells for her disease—blood cells. Somatic cells are cells that, like blood cells, aren't involved in reproduction, so if Ashanti has children, they'll inherit their genes from among the pool that Ashanti was born with, not the version that French Anderson and his colleagues injected into her blood.

Altering the genes of a person before he or she is born is in some ways actually easier than doing so after birth. It's easier to get a gene into every one of a small number of cells than into a large number. At early stages of development, there's no immune system in the embryo to respond in potentially dangerous ways to the gene vector. So as medical motivations drive improvements and innovations in gene therapy, they will also tend to drive germline genetic engineering. As researchers increase the safety and effectiveness of somatic gene therapy through new and better gene vectors, indirectly they'll be making genetic engineering safer and more effective as well.

There are already proposals for procedures that would blur the line between somatic gene therapy and germline engineering. In 1998, French Anderson proposed in utero gene therapy. His idea was to perform gene therapy on a few-weeks- to few-months-old fetus suffering from a genetic ailment, while the fetus was still in its mother's womb. The Recombinant Advisory Commission, the watchdog that looks over all uses of genetic technology in the United States, turned down the request. The commission was concerned that if gene therapy were performed during prenatal development, the inserted genes might find their way to the child's sex organs and then be passed down to future generations.

Genes and the Future of Medicine

Contemporary genome research will be an incalculable resource for the future of medicine. Also, many gene mutations that cause diseases have been identified and used as a basis for clinical diagnosis. Annually, 7.6 million children are born with a severe genetic disorder or birth defect, with 93 percent of these infants born in the developing world. There is abundant evidence that inborn errors of metabolism and inherited conditions such as blood disorders (thalassaemia, hemophilia, sickle cell disorder) could be controlled.

Significant progress has also been made in understanding the genetic basis of multi-factorial diseases and common chronic diseases such as cardiovascular disease, cancer, diabetes, the major psychoses, dementia, rheumatic disease, asthma, and many others. Researchers believe that the information generated by genomics will, in the long term, yield major benefits for many of these diseases and hence the development of completely new approaches to prevention and therapy. Researchers have already identified some of the genes responsible for drug resistance in pathogens leading to tuberculosis, AIDS, and malaria. The diagnosis of leishmaniasis and dengue fever has already been improved by the use of polymerase chain reaction (PCR) [DNA amplification] and non-radioactive DNA probes.

"Interview with Lee Jong-Wook,"
Harvard International Review, *Summer 2004.*

Despite this, there are medical reasons to think about the feasibility of in utero gene therapy. Most children are still conceived the old-fashioned way, through sex rather than IVF. In these children, there's no chance to do genetic screening or alteration before the embryo implants in the womb. But around 3 percent of all pregnancies result in a child with a birth defect of one sort or other, the most common being congenital heart defects, to which several genes have been found to contribute.

Increasingly, concern around the health of unborn children has led to prenatal genetic testing. In the United States, around 13 percent of all expectant mothers go through some form of prenatal genetic test during pregnancy. Amniocentesis, the best known of these procedures, is now recommended for any expectant mother over the age of thirty-five, or for those with a history of Down syndrome or other genetic disorder in their family.

In January 2004, a team of researchers and physicians from the University of California at San Francisco (UCFS) and Washington University published a paper in the British journal *The Lancet* recommending that all mothers undergo amniocentesis or another prenatal genetic test. The team, led by Miriam Kuppermann of UCSF, weighed the pros and cons in economic terms. Amniocentesis has a cost, and it also carries with it a 0.25 to 0.50 percent risk of miscarriage. On the other hand, it can help identify Down syndrome and other problems early in a pregnancy. The total savings to society by early detection of fetal illness, Kuppermann showed, outweighed the cost and risk of the procedure.

What's more, newer tests like CVS (chorionic villi sampling) are less expensive and can be performed earlier in the pregnancy. These tests can pinpoint quite a few genetic diseases, including some that do irreversible harm before birth. For example, Tay-Sachs disease does permanent damage to the brain during gestation. In the near future, prenatal tests will be able to detect Tay-Sachs while an embryo is just a few weeks old.

By performing gene therapy early in a pregnancy, doctors could potentially eliminate Tay-Sachs, cystic fibrosis, congenital heart problems, or other genetic diseases before they have a chance to harm the child. And because the embryo is still rapidly developing, any genes inserted during the pregnancy will be spread through more of the body. In effect, the earlier gene therapy is performed, the easier it is.

For now, the Recombinant Advisory Commission's ruling effectively forbids in utero gene therapy. Yet as genetic testing becomes faster, easier, and more common, more prospective parents will find out that their unborn children bear some genetic disease. Those parents will be looking for ways to cure those diseases as soon as possible.

In utero gene therapy offers such a route. And despite widespread unease about genetic technologies, most Americans seem willing to employ them for medical uses. In a 2002 survey of more than twelve hundred people, the Johns Hopkins University Genetics and Public Policy Center found that 73 percent approved of the use of PGD to preempt genetic disease. The same poll found that 59 percent of Americans approved of the use of genetic engineering to eliminate disease genes from the unborn. . . .

| *"Although scientists have been searching for more than 15 years, and the genetic suspects are legion, the genes responsible for most brain disorders remain unknown."*

Science Surrounding Genetic Testing for Psychiatric Disorders Is Still Evolving

Harvard Mental Health Letter

The following viewpoint, from the Harvard Mental Health Letter, *states that commercial "genetic tests," which allegedly assess an individual's risk of developing a mental or other disorder, are hardly as accurate as their promoters claim. The author claims that serious researchers believe that in most cases, the interplay between genes, rather than any one gene, is responsible for a disorder, and the factors involved are usually too complex to promise easy diagnosis anytime in the near future. The* Harvard Mental Health Letter, *a monthly periodical of current mental health news, is published by the doctors and researchers at Harvard Medical School.*

Harvard Mental Health Letter, "Psychiatric Genetic Tests Raise Concerns," vol. 24, May 2008, p. 4. Copyright © 2008 Harvard University. Republished with permission of Harvard University. For more information visit: www.health.harvard.edu/mental.

As you read, consider the following questions:

1. According to the authors, what is one gene that *has* been accurately linked to a specific brain disorder?
2. What percent of "candidate genes" for causing disorders does one analysis estimate are "false positives"?
3. How many genes make up the "area" that, according to the Autism Genetic Resource Exchange, increases susceptibility to autism?

It is now possible to pay for a commercial genetic test that the company claims will assess the risk of developing bipolar disorder. An individual can register on the company's Web site and pay the required $399 fee, and the company will ship a testing kit to the person's home. The individual requesting the test provides a saliva sample and ships the kit back to the company for analysis. The results are sent to whatever physician a person has designated, who is then expected to communicate the results.

And this is only the beginning. In the next year or two, genetic tests for major depression and schizophrenia are also expected to reach the market. Meanwhile, other companies are racing to develop technology to make sequencing an individual's genome affordable enough that people can learn whether they have gene variants that have been linked to particular diseases, including psychiatric disorders.

Is this the brave new world of genetics and patient empowerment—or a New Age version of snake oil?

Far from an Exact Science

At this point, probably the latter. Although scientists have been searching for more than 15 years, and the genetic suspects are legion, the genes responsible for most brain disorders remain unknown. (A notable exception is a variant of the APOE gene that increases risk for Alzheimer's.) Indeed, when it comes to commercial genetic tests, the age-old advice applies: Let the buyer beware.

Don't Buy a Genetic Test

Genetic testing to identify alleged risk factors that have no proven corrective measures is a waste of money. As noted by Helen Wallace, Ph.D., Deputy Director of GeneWatch UK [a public interest group dedicated to investigation of genetic technologies]: "For most people, tailoring your diet to your genetic make-up is about as scientific as tailoring your diet to your star sign." There is also the concern that without proper regulation, genetic testing could be used to expand the drug market to healthy people who are said to be at high genetic risk. Many people could receive unnecessary medication and suffer the associated adverse effects. Finally, the underlying causes of heart disease, cancer, obesity, adult-onset diabetes, and other diseases might well be ignored, with serious implications for future health.

Stephen Barrett and Harriet Hall, "Dubious Genetic Testers,"
GeneWatch, March-April 2005. www.gene-watch.org.

One problem is that the field of genetics is advancing so rapidly that it's hard to keep up with new developments, never mind figure out which ones may be clinically relevant. One study, for example, found that fewer than 25 percent of psychiatrists felt competent to talk about genetic information with patients and families, and yet 83 percent thought it was their job to do so. . . .

Multiple Genes, Small Impact

The first disease genes ever identified were those for conditions like Huntington's disease, which results from mutations in a single gene. Anyone who inherits that gene develops the disease.

But most experts believe that psychiatric disorders develop because of the interplay between multiple genes, each exerting relatively small effects. That makes finding the responsible genes harder, because there are multiple small targets rather [than] a single relatively large one.

Further complicating matters, research has revealed that many healthy relatives of people with psychiatric disorders have so-called risk genes—and yet do not develop the disorders themselves. Whether or not a person develops an illness depends on unknown ways the risk genes interact with other genes and environmental factors.

False Positives Are Common

Scientists have now identified hundreds, perhaps thousands, of candidate genes that may contribute to schizophrenia, bipolar disorder, and other psychiatric conditions. But experts continue to debate which genes are actually involved.

One problem is that most candidate genes identified fail to hold up—meaning that the association between the gene and a given illness disappears when scientists try to replicate the results from an initial study in a different group of people. One analysis estimated that 70 percent to 80 percent of candidate genes are just such false positives. Thus, one criticism of the psychiatric genetic tests that will first reach the market is that they test for genes that are not proven to be involved in disorders such as depression or schizophrenia.

Where the Science Is Headed

Scientists are optimistic that a genome-wide approach will help better identify the genes involved in psychiatric disorders. This approach recently identified a cluster of genes that affect the risk of developing coronary artery disease and diabetes—which, like psychiatric disorders, arise from the interplay of multiple genes and environmental influences. But a major challenge is that researchers must recruit thousands, and perhaps tens of thousands, of participants in order to find reliable genetic patterns that indicate risk.

The effort has already begun. One example is the Autism Genetic Resource Exchange, a joint effort by researchers collaborating in the Autism Consortium. They reported earlier this year that they had identified a 25-gene area on chromosome 16 that, when deleted or duplicated, increases susceptibility to developing autism. A genetic microarray test that examines the 25 genes at once is now being used at several academic medical centers as part of the diagnostic process to evaluate children suspected of having autism.

Someday it may indeed be possible to reliably assess risk for psychiatric disorders. But at this point, the technology—and the science—is still evolving.

"'This is the future. We need to understand how [stem cells work] and then try and develop therapies from the information that we gather through the research in the laboratories.'"

Stem Cell Research Is Vital to Finding Cures for Genetic Disorders

John Greenwald and Jayne Mackta

Jayne Mackta is president of the New Jersey Association for Biomedical Research, an organizer of New Jersey's Citizens Coalition for Cures which advocates stem cell research, and the mother of a woman with Gaucher's disease, which is a genetic disorder that causes bone ailments, organ swelling, and pulmonary hypertension. In the following interview with John Greenwald of njbiz, Mackta describes the Citizens Coalition's purpose and goals, and argues for increased funding and decreased restrictions on stem cell research. John Greenwald is former managing editor of njbiz, a New Jersey business journal.

As you read, consider the following questions:

1. What are some of the health organizations that make up the Citizens Coalition?

John Greenwald and Jayne Mackta, "A Mother Discusses Stem Cell Research," *njbiz*, vol. 18, February 21, 2005, p. 13. Reproduced by permission.

2. According to Mackta, why are "big pharmas" attracted to New Jersey?

3. Embryos used in stem cell research are about how old?

*J**ohn Greenwald: What is the role of the Citizens Coalition?***

Jayne Mackta: The purpose is to do significant public education about the process of stem cell research. Until we have an informed populace, we're never going to be able to have the support of the legislators and the people who would be making a decision about whether there's a bond issue or not. And while there is certainly some question as to whether there would be a bond issue for stem cell research this year [2005], the coalition is in place to make sure that New Jersey does not miss an opportunity to be a player in this very important field.

How large is the coalition?

It is an organization of voluntary health groups like the Parkinson's Alliance, the Diabetes Association, the Christopher Reeve Paralysis Association and the Brain Injury Association. We're working a coalition of about 40 or 50 organizations and more are coming on as we formalize it.

Increased Support

What is your role in the coalition?

As president of the New Jersey Association of Biomedical Research it's my role to make sure that [the coalition] happens.

How does the proposed [Acting Governor of New Jersey, Richard] Codey initiative play into this?

When the governor announced his intention to seek more support for stem cell research in New Jersey, several leaders of nonprofits were gathered together and I was included in the group. So it was in response to his vision and the leadership that he exerted from the very beginning for the legislation for

Adult Stem Cells

Last year [2007], researchers developed the ability to convert adult cells into stem cells. . . .

As the genes involved in adult-onset disorders are often dispensable for stem cell growth, most diseases can be studied by the use of DSCs [disease stem cells]. Once in the stem cell state, DSCs ensure that an indefinite supply of the relevant tissue can be generated.

John Timmer, "Disease-Specific Stem Cells to Boost Research,"
August 11, 2008. http://arstechnica.com.

the Stem Cell Institute [of New Jersey] [to be located in New Brunswick] that we have become much more focused. [The Institute's groundbreaking was in October 2007.] It seems that whenever people have the opportunity to understand how stem cells work they recognize that this is something good and important for the health of the people, not only of people in New Jersey but around the world.

Maintaining the Lead

Are you worried that Codey's initiative could die since he has decided not to seek a full term as governor?

We're hoping that it won't. This initiative is not only about health, it's about the economic health of New Jersey as well. [In November 2007, the initiative, which would have appropriated $450 million in bonds to finance stem cell research, was defeated by New Jersey voters.] It would be really unfortunate if we did not take advantage of the many opportunities and the constellation of wonderful resources already here in New Jersey.

Based on what?

It's based on the outstanding researchers who are leaders in the field and many other people who are doing stem cell work already. They can come to New Jersey, and they will come if we have the infrastructure set up for them. It's critically important that we maintain the lead that we have, building on the collaboration that we've already been able to contribute and having the possibility of well-known researchers coming to New Jersey. It's the way we feed the big pharmas, because they've always found researchers in our academic institutions who have fed into their pipelines. If we don't have the brightest and the best we may see more big companies leave New Jersey.

A Great Network

How will the coalition's campaign work?

We have a great network through the voluntary organizations that are part of this. They have not only patients but families and caregivers and extended families. So it will be a multifaceted campaign where we'll be having articles for their newsletters and materials for their Web sites, and there will be a real increase in the level of noise, if you will, about the progress and promise of stem cell research.

Does that include embryonic stem cell research? President Bush and some religious groups oppose it because it kills the embryo. That's different from the stem cells taken from umbilical cord blood or adult organs.

They all serve a little different purpose, but the way research works best is that you have the opportunity to explore the possibilities of all methodologies. For a very short window of time a very few cells in the growing embryo have the ability to turn into any kind of cell. Once they start differentiating they start to become, say, skin cells or respiratory cells. Nobody knows the extent to which we can really utilize those cells, but they hold tremendous promise. And the reasons that we're searching for different mechanisms is that we've always been dependent for the last century on using surgery and medicines to cure and treat diseases. This is a new science. This is the future. We need to understand how it works and then try and develop therapies from the information that we gather through the research in the laboratories. And if we're not allowed to go down a certain road, who knows what tremendous opportunities we may miss?

Ethical Issues

How do embryonic stem cells differ from adult stem cells?

There are stem cells in adult parts of the body that can replicate, but only into what they already are. [In 2007, medical researchers developed a technique to give adult cells the properties of embryonic stem cells—see sidebar.] There are stem cells in the heart; they're finding them in the major organs and body systems.

Can there be a middle ground between the proponents and opponents of embryonic stem cell research?

There is no middle ground for people who believe that life begins at conception. For them the 4- or 5-day-old embryo that is no bigger than the head of a pin represents a baby. The scientific community and people who do not agree with that definition believe that if you take the stem cells that are formed at that very early stage, in a 4- or 5-day-old embryo, you are putting them in a petri dish. You are not talking about a baby. Those cells will never grow into a baby. [Researchers] can retrieve those stem cells and they very rapidly reproduce, and that's how they generate those stem cell lines that the federal government has said that people can use.

> *"Embryonic cell research [in itself] . . . that destroys an embryo, puts it at unnecessary or material risk, and/or creates clones or embryos . . . genetically manipulated to terminate . . . poses serious ethical problems."*

Embryonic Stem Cell Research Poses Ethical Considerations

William Sutherland

In the following viewpoint, author William Sutherland argues that while embryonic stem cell research is not invariably unethical, harming or discarding the embryos is, since, containing the full genetic material necessary to grow into adults, they are in effect human beings whose lives are as valuable as those that might be saved through the research's discoveries. The author advocates further development of alternate research techniques, including the manipulation of single cells, messenger chemicals, and human eggs to produce stem cells and tissue. Sutherland is a writer and a member of the International Poetry Hall of Fame.

As you read, consider the following questions:

1. How many cells make up a human blastomere?
2. According to Sutherland, why is every life "inviolable"?
3. In a Japanese study, what four messenger chemicals were used to create tissue without embryos?

With well-publicized declarations that embryonic stem cells may be the panacea for every disease and affliction that defies current medical treatments based on surgical procedures and drug-based therapies, vocal support for stem cell research continues to grow louder. Proponents emphatically state that such research could regenerate failing organs since they have the potential to "become nerve cells, muscle cells, heart cells and all of the other cells in the body" and cure diseases and other afflictions such as Alzheimer's disease, diabetes, macular degeneration and even blindness, multiple sclerosis, Parkinson's disease and spinal cord injuries. In the rush to justify and promote this research, ethical questions such as "Do embryonic stem cells represent a life, should 'extra' frozen embryos created through in vitro fertilization be used to establish stem cell lines, and does the end (potential for and even cures of debilitating diseases and afflictions) justify the means (human embryonic stem cell research even if the embryo is destroyed in the process)?" are pushed aside. Worse yet, research has even been distorted, exaggerated and/or fabricated to promote embryonic stem cell research. . . .

It Is Doubtful That a Single Cell Has Potential Life

Presently there is no evidence that a single stem cell, once replication has begun, has "the intrinsic capacity to generate a complete organism in any mammalian species" when extracted during the blastomere stage (when the fetus is two-days old and consists of eight cells), Dr. Robert Lanza, a scientist at Advanced Cell Technology, stated. Yet critics argue that the potential does exist presenting an ethical dilemma that can only be resolved through scientific research. Accordingly, it is imperative that scientists who already extract a single cell from a human blastomere for PGD (preimplantation genetic diagnosis) during in vitro fertilization to test for genetic disorders, replicate this cell prior to testing and conduct research to determine if it indeed can create an embryo and thus a life, on its own. However, unless proven otherwise, it is doubtful that a single cell extracted during the blastomere stage constitutes nor can create a life any more than during any stage following fertilization and replication from the initial single cell. Otherwise much if not all medical research and procedures (e.g. blood testing, organ transplants, etc.) would be morally unethical since they would involve the destruction of life or potential life.

Embryos Should Not Be Destroyed

It is clear that "'extra' frozen embryos created through in vitro fertilization" should not be used to establish stem cell lines, especially since they are in the blastocyst stage (consisting 150 or more cells) and any such extraction will destroy the fetus and ultimately a human life. Even arguments that stem cells should be extracted since couples responsible for the said embryos have ordered their destruction remain inconsistent and indefensible. Such originating instructions by and of themselves are unethical and morally reprehensible. As a matter of fact, each frozen embryo should be made available for implantation so that a human life is permitted to develop to its full potential in lieu of perpetual stasis or destruction.

Consistent with the above premise, the Church of Scotland explicitly states "human dignity inheres in the very existence of the embryo . . . it has the full genetic complement of a human being, which neither egg nor sperm possessed separately," reinforced by the *Catechism of the Catholic Church*, "Human life must be respected and protected absolutely from the moment of conception. From the moment of existence, a human being must be recognized as having the rights of a person—among which is the inviolable right of every innocent being to life."

A Life for a Life?

The third question poses additional ethical challenges since it also attempts to discern the value of a life itself. When focusing on embryonic stem cell research that may destroy one life to save another—the end justifying the means, the value of two lives is compared, a proposition that has been the subject of philosophical, theological, and scientific discussion for centuries. "Is one life more valuable than another and is one life worth saving at the expense of another?"

When these arguments are viewed, the end (saving of one life) can never justify the means when it involves the taking of another life (destruction of a blastocyst fetus to extract embryonic stem cells) when the life taken has not posed an imminent threat to the life saved, the basis of self-defense. When the debate about when life begins is put aside, Judeo-Christian tradition considers each and every life to be equally sacred and inviolable since "from its beginning it involves the creative action of God and remains for ever in a special relationship with the Creator." This position is further affirmed by the philosopher Josef Popper-Lynkeus who asserts in *Das Individuum und die Bewertung menschlicher Existenzen* that "the existence of a stupid peasant-boy is just as infinitely valuable as the existence of a Shakespeare or a Newton."

All Human Life Is Valuable at Any Stage

In short, "all life is worth living under any condition because of its inherent value . . . since it is intrinsically good, no life is more valuable than another, [and] that lives not fully developed (embryonic and fetal stages) and lives with no great potential (the terminally ill [and] the severely handicapped) are still sacred" whose termination cannot be justified.

All Life Is Sacred

It is difficult to imagine a scenario under which the extraction technique [for removing embryonic stem cells without harming the embryo itself], even if perfected, could be implemented on a large enough scale to provide the number of stem cells needed for research without leading to the cultivation of embryos for the express purpose of destroying them. There is the eugenic intention. Unless scientists can guarantee a womb for each embryo from whom single cells are safely extracted (which is not currently done in the context of pre-implantation genetic testing), then the protection against deliberate destruction of life afforded by this proposed technique is illusory. . . .

I am willing to accept a bright-line limit on how far I will let my empathy and hope for a medical cure take me—I will not accept the deliberate destruction of embryos.

My experience as a parent [of a son with Down syndrome] and as a Catholic bears on my willingness to accept such a limit. As I see it, the image and likeness of God reflected in every life, including embryonic life, includes conditions like Down syndrome, autism and Parkinson's disease. To look for cures that deny the sacredness of all human life is to reject the aspect of God's image reflected in conditions society deems disabling.

Elizabeth R. Schiltz, "The Disabled Jesus,"
America, *March 12, 2007.*

Accordingly, embryonic stem cell research is [in itself] neither incompatible nor unethical. Only such research that destroys an embryo, puts it at unnecessary or material risk, and/or creates clones or embryos even if they are genetically manipulated to terminate at a given time in their developmental state before birth, poses serious ethical problems.

However, not all embryonic stem cell research presents moral hurdles. Today technology is evolving that permits the creation of embryonic stem cells without embryonic destruction. A project by Advanced Cell Technology, a Massachusetts biotech company, successfully created embryonic stem cells from a single cell that had been removed from an 8-cell blastomere mouse embryo.

When it comes to humans, laboratories already extract a single cell from an 8-cell blastomere to test for chromosomal abnormalities prior to implantation. Therefore because of this PGD test, such a cell could be extracted and then cultivated overnight into additional embryonic stem cells prior to testing, posing a negligible risk to the fetus. As this test is already conducted and to date has resulted in no adverse effects, it is ethically acceptable and even obligatory to expand upon the PGD test to create embryonic stem cells that can be used for scientific research and ultimately to treat debilitating diseases and afflictions.

Tissue Without Embryos

Next, in a second study, Japanese scientists at the University of Kyoto, Shinya Yamanaka and Kazutoshi Takahashi, created "all kinds of tissue types without the use of embryos" by exposing mouse skin cells to Oct3/4, Sox2, c-Myc and Klf4, "four messenger chemicals found in embryonic cells."

Third, though not tested or proven, a member of the President's Council on Bioethics has offered another alternative to avoid embryonic destruction. He proposed "a technique, called 'altered nuclear transfer,' that would genetically engineer an egg (which it has been established does not constitute a life) so that it is incapable of becoming an embryo, but can still produce embryonic stem cells."

The Need for Further Development

Therefore as scientific research progresses and new technology evolves, embryonic stem cell research can be harnessed to its full potential overcoming ethical barriers, namely the destruction of one human life to save another. However, it must be noted that despite optimistic promises, embryonic stem cell research is still in its infancy with a lot to be done. Even once embryonic stem cells can be produced in quantity overcoming the inefficiency of today's methods and potential problems (e.g. efficacy of viruses in implanted cells, use of c-Myc that is known to play a role in the progression of cancer), further research will be needed to determine and provide the correct instructions for an embryonic stem cell to grow into its desired pathway (e.g. neurons, rods and cones, a liver, myocardial muscle, etc.). Only then will replacement tissue be generated, overcoming organ shortages and possible immuno-rejection that will give individuals a new lease on life. As a result, "many scientists have begun to back off from the field's extravagant promises" and consider it a long-term project whose "horizon is as many as 15 to 20 years away" leading to Gordon Keller's (appointed Director of the McEwen Centre for Regenerative Medicine in Toronto, Canada, whose term commences in 2007) cautionary words, "We need to be careful that we're not overselling the immediate potential" of embryonic stem cells. However, once ethical concerns are overcome through research and new technology, the time frame from promise to treatment may accelerate as many major pharmaceutical and biotechnology firms that have stayed away, enter the field leading to increased life spans and enhanced quality of life.

Periodical Bibliography

The following articles have been selected to supplement the diverse views presented in this chapter.

Jane Bainbridge	"Screening Eggs for Abnormalities: Hope for Childless Couples?" *British Journal of Midwifery*, March 2007.
Patrick Barry	"Finding the Golden Genes," *Science News*, August 2, 2008.
Shaoni Bhattacharya and Sylvia Pagán	"A New Role for Stem Cells," *New Scientist*, June 19, 2004.
John George	"Children's Hospital Will Debut $20M Special Delivery Unit," *Philadelphia Business Journal*, May 16, 2008.
Edmund S. Higgins	"The New Genetics of Mental Illness," *Scientific American Mind*, 2008.
John Merriman	"Genetic Risk Factors for MS Identified," *Neurology Reviews*, September 2007.
Andrew Pollack	"Drug Makers Seek Clues to Side Effects in Genes," *New York Times*, September 27, 2007.
Shari Roan	"Gene Therapy May Reverse Down Syndrome," *Houston Chronicle*, October 16, 2003.
Sally Sara	"For People with Down Syndrome, Longer Life Has Complications," *New York Times*, June 1, 2008.
Nancy Shute	"What Will Human Beings Become?" *U.S. News & World Report*, August 4, 2008.
Emily Singer	"Stem Cells Reborn," *Technology Review*, May 2006.
Bob Smietana	"When Does Personhood Begin?" *Christianity Today*, July 2004.

For Further Discussion

Chapter 1

1. Lee Bowman, drawing on March of Dimes research, emphasizes the many cases of genetic disorders throughout the world. Richard H. Carmona, also speaking in relation to March of Dimes materials, believes that such disorders are decreasing and will continue to do so. Do you think genetic disorder incidents are increasing or decreasing? Why? What are some possible reasons, besides those mentioned in the selections, for changes in the number of disorders reported?

2. Penelope Ross and Monica Cuskelly take an academic approach to the difficulties facing families that include children with mental or emotional disabilities; John C. McGinley talks about his personal joys in raising a son with Down syndrome. Do you think professional but impersonal research or personal experience has greater value?

Chapter 2

1. Susan Brink emphasizes the growing acceptance of people with genetic disorders in everyday life. Karen Kaplan, however, focuses on the problem of genetic discrimination, particularly the U.S. military's denial of medical benefits on the basis of "bad genes." Both authors are experienced health writers, but they focus here on life in different areas of society. In your opinion, are social and business atmospheres in general becoming more or less favorable to people with genetic disorders? What evidence supports your answer?

2. Fred E. Foldvary emphasizes the potential expenses involved in dealing with genetic disorders and says that

family, not society, should pay nearly all expenses. The Westchester Arc viewpoint, by contrast, emphasizes the potential value to society when people with genetic and other developmental disorders become full and productive members. How much do you think the larger society should be expected to invest in the care and education of people with developmental disorders? Support your answer.

3. Mark Richert argues that standard educational practices focus on the principle of giving children with disabilities all possible contact with other children, but at the expense of ignoring individual interests. Joetta Sack-Min, while agreeing that extra difficulties are involved, presents arguments for integrating classes to the greatest extent possible. Which argument do you find more persuasive? Noting that each viewpoint focuses on a different disorder, how far do you think the nature of a disorder should figure into choosing the best options for individual students?

Chapter 3

1. Bruce K. Lin and Alan R. Fleischman argue in favor of routine testing for newborns on a wide variety of genetic disorders. Do you think that genetic disorders should be routinely tested for as early as possible in the pregnancy, immediately after birth, or only on parental request? Support your answer.

2. Amy Harmon reports the viewpoints of several people who chose abortion as a legitimate, though heartbreaking, option when a fetus was found to have a genetic disorder. Patricia E. Bauer argues against aborting fetuses with Down syndrome. Do you think that abortion is *generally* an acceptable means of preventing genetic disorders? Why or why not? What criteria do you think should be considered in determining the proper course of action for *individual* cases?

3. Ramesh Ponnuru argues that increased genetic screening encourages "eugenic" attitudes because it fuels subtle, and not-so-subtle, pressure to abort fetuses with genetic disorders. Ruth Schwartz Cowan, by contrast, says that there are fundamental differences—notably an increase in universal freedom of reproduction—between medical genetics and eugenics. Which argument do you find more persuasive? Why?

Chapter 4

1. Ronald M. Green focuses on the potential benefits of gene engineering and considers the potential problems to be surmountable. Jim Manzi, on the other hand, expresses concern that an obsession with genes will turn into attitudes of simplification and superiority (the latter of which Green brushes aside). Do you think that the potential benefits of learning to manipulate genes outweigh the difficulties and risks? Why or why not?

2. Ramez Naam sees a future where in utero gene therapy may be able to treat nearly all genetic disorders in the earliest stages of fetal development. The *Harvard Mental Health Letter*, by contrast, emphasizes that—contrary to the claims of many companies pushing commercial genetic testing—the genetic factors behind many disorders are still far from being understood. How soon, if ever, do you think medical science will be able to fix most genetic flaws before birth? Defend your answer.

3. Jayne Mackta argues that the embryos used in stem cell research are not yet human beings and that the research is important to finding cures for genetic and other disorders. William Sutherland says that the embryos *are* human beings, but that there are ways to conduct stem cell research without harming them. In deciding which view is more credible, keep in mind that Mackta has a child with a ge-

netic disorder and Sutherland is speaking from a strongly religious viewpoint and consider how the objectivity of each may be affected.

Organizations to Contact

The editors have compiled the following list of organizations concerned with the issues debated in this book. The descriptions are derived from materials provided by the organizations. All have publications or information available for interested readers. The list was compiled on the date of publication of the present volume; the information provided here may change. Be aware that many organizations take several weeks or longer to respond to inquiries, so allow as much time as possible.

American Association of People with Disabilities (AAPD)
1629 K Street NW, Suite 503, Washington, DC   20006
(800) 840-8844
Web site: www.aapd-dc.org

The American Association of People with Disabilities (AAPD) is the largest nonprofit cross-disability member organization in the United States. Its purpose is to encourage economic self-sufficiency and political voice for the 50 million Americans with disabilities. AAPD is an active advocate for disability nondiscrimination laws. It publishes a quarterly newsletter, *AAPD News*, and its Web site posts numerous disability-related articles.

**American College of Obstetricians
and Gynecologists (ACOG)**
409 Twelfth Street SW, PO Box 96920
Washington, DC   20090-6920
(202) 638-5577
E-mail: resources@acog.org
Web site: www.acog.org

The American College of Obstetricians and Gynecologists (ACOG) is the leading United States organization for women's health care professionals. Founded in 1951, it has over fifty-two thousand members and serves as an advocate for patient education, high medical standards, and awareness of current issues. It publishes a variety of educational pamphlets—including *Genetic Disorders* and *7 Things Parents Want to Know About Newborn Screening*—and the newsletters *ACOG Today* and *ACOG Committee Opinion*, the latter of which has featured articles on issues such as genetic testing.

Centers for Disease Control and Prevention (CDC)
1600 Clifton Road, Atlanta, GA   30333
(800) 232-4636
E-mail: cdcinfo@cdc.gov
Web site: www.cdc.gov

The Centers for Disease Control and Prevention (CDC), a major branch of the U.S. government's Department of Health and Human Services, is the country's primary federal public health agency. It manages, among other entities, the National Institute for Occupational Safety and Health. The CDC maintains an electronic library, which receives some 40 million visitors a month, on its Web site; online articles include "Risk Factors for Down Syndrome [Trisomy 21]," "Family History Is Important for Your Health," and "Living Well with Sickle Cell Disease."

Comment on Reproductive Ethics (CORE)
PO BOX 4593, London   SW3 6XE
   England
00 44 (0)207 581 2623 • Fax: 00 44 (0)207 581 3868
E-mail: info@corethics.org
Web site: www.corethics.org

Founded in 1994, Comment on Reproductive Ethics (CORE) is a pro-life public interest group dedicated to fostering balanced public debate on the ethical issues surrounding reproductive technology and to protecting the welfare of children conceived by new methods. Opposed to human cloning and abortion, as well as to any stem cell research that involves embryo destruction, the group posts a variety of relevant editorials on the "press releases" page of its Web site.

Council for Responsible Genetics (CRG)
5 Upland Road, Suite 3, Cambridge, MA   02140
(617) 868-0870 • Fax: (617) 491-5344
E-mail: crg@gene-watch.org
Web site: www.gene-watch.org

The Council for Responsible Genetics (CRG) fosters public education and debate about the ethical, social, and environmental implications of genetic technology. It publishes *GeneWatch* magazine, the country's premier periodical on biotechnological ethics, and maintains an online bookstore whose titles include *Rights and Liberties in the Biotech Age: Why We Need a Genetic Bill of Rights* and *The Dream of the Perfect Child.*

Easter Seals
230 West Monroe, Suite 1800, Chicago, IL   60606
(800) 221-6827
Web site: www.easterseals.com

Easter Seals, founded in 1919 as the National Society for Crippled Children, was the first major advocacy and support organization for those with disabilities. It took its current name, formally adopted in 1967, from the postal seals, marked with an Easter lily logo, it provided to donors. Easter Seals currently employs some thirteen thousand people, maintains over five hundred and fifty branch offices, and serves over a million children and adults with disabilities. Its services include physical and occupational therapy, day care, recreational programs, and anti-discrimination lobbying e-articles and booklets on a variety of "coping with disabilities" topics, including "Transportation Solutions for Caregivers," "Easy Access Housing for Easier Living," and "Myths and Facts about People with Disabilities," that can be accessed through the Web site.

GeneTests
9725 Third Avenue NE, Suite 602, Seattle, WA   98115
(206) 616-4033 • Fax: (206) 221-4679

E-mail: genetest@u.washington.edu
Web site: www.genetests.org

Funded by the National Institutes of Health, GeneTests is a publicly funded medical genetics information resource for researchers and health care professionals. Its primary mission is to promote the responsible use of genetic services through the provision of up-to-date information on genetic testing and counseling; and it publishes *GeneReviews,* an online collection of expert-written articles on the role of genetic testing in diagnosing disease. The Web site has an extensive online glossary of genetic terms, and an "About Genetic Services" information section.

March of Dimes Foundation
1275 Mamaroneck Avenue, White Plains, NY   10605
(914) 997-4488
Web site: www.marchofdimes.com

The March of Dimes is a leading nonprofit organization and a major advocate for pregnancy and newborn health, focused on preventing birth defects and infant mortality. Founded in 1921 in response to polio epidemics, the foundation now focuses on a variety of causes including public education, affordable health insurance, the prevention of premature births, and genetic research. Its "Birth Defects and Genetic Conditions" Web page has nearly two dozen articles on various disorders as well as materials on genetic research and counseling. The March of Dimes also publishes a monthly e-newsletter, archived on its Web site.

**National Center for Education in Maternal
and Child Health (NCEMCH)**
Georgetown University, Washington, DC   20057
(202) 687-0100
Web site: www.ncemch.org

The National Center for Education in Maternal and Child Health (NCEMCH) was established in 1982 as a national resource of program development and public education for the health and well-being of children and families. NCEMCH collaborates with a broad range of government agencies, corporate and philanthropic partners, professional organizations, and academic institutions on national health initiatives. Its online library includes a "Genetics" section with numerous links to e-newsletters and other resources; NCEMCH also publishes the weekly e-newsletter *MCH Alert*, on current news in the field.

National Human Genome Research Institute
National Institutes of Health, Bethesda, MD   20892-2152
(301) 402-0911 • Fax: (301) 402-2218
Web site: www.genome.gov

The National Human Genome Research Institute (NHGRI) was established in 1989 as the National Center for Human Genome Research (NCHGR), the National Institutes of Health's representative in the International Human Genome Project. The agency received its current name in 1997. Its Web site's Educational Resources page includes links to a variety of topics on genetic disorders and other genetic research issues.

National Institutes of Health
9000 Rockville Pike, Bethesda, MD   20892
(301) 496-4000
E-mail: NIHinfo@od.nih.gov
Web site: www.nih.gov

The National Institutes of Health (NIH), a branch of the U.S. Department of Health and Human Services, conducts and supports an extensive variety of medical research and comprises twenty-seven institutes and centers. The agency traces its roots to the 1887 creation of the Laboratory of Hygiene, Marine Hospital, Staten Island, New York. Its primary purposes today are to foster innovative research strategies to advance the country's public health capacities; to develop and maintain disease prevention resources; to expand medical knowledge to the application of economic well-being; and to promote scientific integrity and public accountability. The agency publishes the *NIH News in Health* newsletter and an online column called "Research Matters"; the Web site also maintains a page of up-to-date medical science press releases.

National Tay-Sachs and Allied Diseases Association (NTSAD)
2001 Beacon Street, Suite 204, Boston, MA   02135
(800) 906-8723 • Fax: (617) 277-0134
Web site: www.ntsad.org

The National Tay-Sachs and Allied Diseases Association (NTSAD) was founded in 1956 by a small group of parents whose children suffered from Tay-Sachs disease and related genetic disorders. The association, an early pioneer in community education, carrier screening, and laboratory quality control programs, has to date conducted over 2 million Tay-Sachs gene tests. NTSAD services now comprise forty-eight different genetic diagnoses. The organization provides extensive Peer Support Group services for its members; its publications include the annual newsletter *Breakthrough*, the bimonthly *Late Onset Tay-Sachs Community Newsletter*, and a variety of educational pamphlets and booklets including *What Is Tay-Sachs?* and *The Home Care Book*.

Nemours Foundation
4600 Touchton Road East, Jacksonville, FL   32246
(904) 232-4100 • Fax: (904) 232-4125
Web site: www.nemours.org

Nemours is one of the nation's largest children's health institutions, employing over four thousand professionals, including nearly four hundred and fifty specialists. Dedicated to providing care and programs not readily available elsewhere, especially for families with limited financial resources, it describes its vision as "Freedom from Disabling Conditions." It owns and operates the Alfred I. duPont Hospital for Children and the Nemours Children's Clinic, and maintains the KidsHealth Web site (www.kidshealth.org) with sections for parents, children, and teens. The KidsHealth site includes online articles on "The Basics on Genes and Genetic Disorders" and on various individual disorders.

NYSARC, Inc.
393 Delaware Avenue, Delmar, NY   12054
(518) 439-8311
E-mail: info@nysarc.org
Web site: www.nysarc.org

Founded in 1949 as a parental advocacy group working for the rights of children with developmental disabilities, NYSARC secured the nation's first legislation to protect the rights of such persons. The organization is dedicated to improving quality of life for those who have mental or developmental retardation from genetic disorders or other medical conditions. The empowerment of families is a primary emphasis. NYSARC publishes the newsletter *Our Voice Today.*

REMEDI (Regenerative Medicine Institute)
National Centre for Biomedical Engineering Science
Galway, Ireland
+353 91 495166
E-mail: info@remedi.ie
Web site: www.remedi.ie

REMEDI, the Regenerative Medicine Institute, is a research institute active in gene and adult stem cell therapy for the purpose of regenerating and repairing body tissues. The institute was established in 2003 through a Science Foundation Ireland (SFI) Centre for Science Engineering and Technology (CSET) award combined with industry funding. REMEDI's partnership of scientists, clinicians, and engineers is dedicated to developing new treatment options. Its Web site includes information on stem cell and genetic research, as well as links to related articles.

Bibliography of Books

Ernest L. Abel   *Jewish Genetic Disorders: A Layman's Guide.* Jefferson, NC: McFarland, 2008.

Melanie Ann Apel   *Cystic Fibrosis: The Ultimate Teen Guide.* Lanham, MD: Scarecrow Press, 2006.

Maria R. Burgio   *Is My Child Normal?: When Behavior Is Okay, When It's Not, How to Tell the Difference, and What to Do Next.* Fort Lee, NJ: Barricade Books, Inc., 2008.

Harold Chen   *Atlas of Genetic Diagnosis and Counseling.* Totowa, NJ: Humana Press, 2006.

Committee on Improving Birth Outcomes   *Reducing Birth Defects: Meeting the Challenge in the Developing World.* Eds. Judith R. Bale, Barbara J. Stoll, and Adetokunbo O. Lucas. Washington, DC: National Academies Press, 2003.

Ruth Schwartz Cowan   *Heredity and Hope: The Case for Genetic Screening.* Cambridge, MA: Harvard University Press, 2008.

Elizabeth Ettorre   *Before Birth: Understanding Prenatal Screening.* Aldershot, UK: Ashgate Publishing Limited, 2001.

Masha Gessen	*Blood Matters: From Inherited Illness to Designer Babies, How the World and I Found Ourselves in the Future of the Gene*. Orlando, FL: Harcourt, 2008.
Ronald Michael Green	*Babies by Design: The Ethics of Genetic Choice*. New Haven, CT: Yale University Press, 2007.
John Harris	*Enhancing Evolution: The Ethical Case for Making Better People*. Princeton, NJ: Princeton University Press, 2007.
Ren Kimura	*Genetic Inheritance Patterns*. New York: Nova Science Publishers, 2008.
Beth Kohl	*Embryo Culture: Making Babies in the Twenty-First Century*. New York: Farrar, Straus and Giroux, 2007.
Sheldon Krimsky and Peter Shorett, eds.	*Rights and Liberties in the Biotech Age: Why We Need a Genetic Bill of Rights*. Lanham, MD: Rowman & Littlefield Publishers, Inc., 2005.
Kate Maloy and Maggie Jones Patterson	*Birth or Abortion: Private Struggles in a Political World*. Jackson, TN: Perseus Books Group, 2002.
Joseph Panno	*Gene Therapy: Treating Disease by Repairing Genes*. New York: Facts on File, 2005.
Juan Martos Pérez	*New Developments in Autism: The Future Is Today*. London: Jessica Kingsley Publishers, 2007.

Oliver Quarrell   *Huntington's Disease: The Facts.*
Oxford, UK: Oxford University Press,
1999.

Philip R. Reilly   *Is It in Your Genes?: The Influence of
Genes on Common Disorders and
Diseases That Affect You and Your
Family.* Cold Spring Harbor, NY:
Cold Spring Harbor Laboratory
Press, 2004.

Roger N.
Rosenberg   *The Molecular and Genetic Basis of
Neurologic and Psychiatric Disease.*
Philadelphia: Wolters Kluwer
Health/Lippincott Williams &
Wilkins, 2008.

Joan Rothschild   *The Dream of the Perfect Child.*
Bloomington: Indiana University
Press, 2005.

Michael Rutter
and the Novartis
Foundation   *Genetic Effects on Environmental
Vulnerability to Disease.* Chicester,
West Sussex, UK: Wiley-Blackwell,
2008.

Pete Shanks   *Human Genetic Engineering: A Guide
for Activists, Skeptics, and the Very
Perplexed.* New York: Nation Books,
2005.

Kathryn Lynard
Soper   *Gifts: Mothers Reflect on How
Children with Down Syndrome Enrich
Their Lives.* Bethesda, MD: Woodbine
House, 2007.

Sandy Sulaiman — *Learning to Live with Huntington's Disease: One Family's Story*. London: Jessica Kingsley Publishers, 2007.

Doris Teichler-Zalen — *To Test or Not to Test: A Guide to Genetic Screening and Risk*. New Brunswick, NJ: Rutgers University Press, 2008.

Judith Tsipis and the National Tay-Sachs and Allied Diseases Association — *What Every Family Should Know*. Boston, MA: National Tay-Sachs & Allied Diseases Association, Inc, 2003.

Sherryl Vint — *Bodies of Tomorrow: Technology, Subjectivity, Science Fiction*. Toronto: University of Toronto Press, 2007.

Keith Wailoo and Stephen Gregory Pemberton — *The Troubled Dream of Genetic Medicine: Ethnicity and Innovation in Tay-Sachs, Cystic Fibrosis, and Sickle Cell Disease*. Baltimore, MD: Johns Hopkins University Press, 2006.

James Wynbrandt — *The Encyclopedia of Genetic Disorders and Birth Defects*. New York: Facts on File, 2008.

Mitchell Zuckoff — *Choosing Naia: A Family's Journey*. Boston, MA: Beacon Press, 2002.

Index